From this day forward

Marriage Equality in Australia:
Where the debate came from
Why the reform matters
How change will be achieved

with some digressions on
Australian history, gay identity and Tasmania

Walleah Press
PO Box 368
North Hobart
Tasmania 7002
Australia

http://walleahpress.com.au
admin@ walleahpress.com.au

ISBN 978-1-877010-68-2

Preface

In 2010, Alison and John Green at Pantera Press asked me to write the case for marriage equality in seven short chapters. They hoped to produce a series of books, titled *Why v Why*, summarising the case for and against particular reforms. The "no" case to my "yes" was provided by Bill Muehlenberg, a conservative religious commentator and self-proclaimed culture warrior. Whereas I saw marriage equality as an affirmation of Australia's core values, Muehlenberg saw it as a threat to them. We agreed to a civil debate free of personal attacks, and to some live discussion on ABC radio. That was all we agreed on.

The assumption behind the original book was that marriage equality divided public opinion and that advocates, for and against, needed to present a persuasive case to win support. My contribution was tailored to that end. It was about convincing those opposed to, or unsure about, marriage equality to support it. I set out to do this by going beyond the catch cry of "equal love" to other, deeper arguments for change. The marriage equality debate has shifted markedly since then. Marriage equality now exists in every developed English-speaking nation apart from Australia. Australian public support for the reform has increased from just below 60 per cent to over 70, one of the highest levels in the world. Indeed, there is now more support for marriage equality than opposition to it in every demographic, including older people and people of faith. The community debate is over. The job at hand is to encourage, inform and skill supporters of marriage equality to voice their support to law makers.

I decided to update, expand and republish what I wrote in response to these new circumstances. I have travelled to every corner of the nation advocating for marriage equality and everywhere I find supporters asking for more information about the reform. They want to know where the current debate originated, which path to marriage equality they should support, and how they can make their voices heard. As in 2010, supporters today want an understanding of the issue that goes beyond catch cries.

The seven chapters written for the original book have been updated and three more added. What amazed me when I was updating this original text, was how much had changed in Australia and overseas in a relatively short period. This has re-ignited my hope that marriage equality can be achieved soon. I have also added several commentaries addressing broader aspects of the debate. In the second section of the book I reflect on where the marriage equality debate came from and how the reform will be achieved. In the third section I digress into the history of freedom to marry in Australia, criticism of marriage equality from the left and what Tasmania's leadership on the issue says about the Island. Because I am no longer constrained by tight word limits and the relentless need to convince a general audience, these commentaries are more nuanced and, at times, personal. Two of these essays were first published elsewhere, inevitably leading to some repetition of ideas. I have tried to keep this to a minimum.

It is impossible for me to anticipate every question supporters of marriage equality might ask, or provide every answer. But I hope the range of topics I cover will at least spur supporters to find out more about the reform they hold dear and to use this knowledge to inform their own advocacy.

I'm grateful to those who helped me with the text, including Mik, Martine, Shirleene, Peter, Ivan and Alex, and to Ralph Wessman at Walleah Press for his interest in the project and his patience with my erratic schedule. Most of all, I am indebted to Rafael for all his love, encouragement and support. Without him this book would not have been possible.

Rodney Croome
Hobart May 2015

A note on language

When this text was originally published in 2010, the term "same-sex marriage" was preferred to "marriage equality" because it was more easily understood by a general audience and it was a term both co-authors could agree to use. I have used "marriage equality" more often in this version because the term is now more familiar. I much prefer "marriage equality" because ultimately there should be no such thing as "same-sex marriage", just "marriage". But where I need to distinguish partners who can't marry from those who can, I have used the terms "same-sex partner", "same-sex couples" and "same-sex marriages". I take these terms to include transgender and intersex people who are currently unable to marry. I acknowledge "same-sex" may not be fully inclusive of those intersex people who do not identify as male or female. But it is the clearest and simplest term currently available to refer to non-heterosexual unions. To describe these unions I have used the terms "different sex" or "other sex" instead of "opposite-sex". This avoids overstating the differences between men and women.

Contents

DIGRESSIONS FROM THE MARRIAGE EQUALITY DEBATE

WHY SAME-SEX COUPLES SHOULD

BE ALLOWED TO MARRY

Introduction to section one

In the first section of this book, I outline the main reasons for allowing same-sex couples to marry.

For many supporters of marriage equality their case is obvious. The words "fairness", "equity", "respect" and, above all, "love", occur frequently in the everyday conversations, talk-back radio calls, and letters-to-the-editor, explaining the need for reform.

But marriage equality is about more than these heartfelt values, as important as they are.

Allowing same-sex couples the right to marry is crucial to removing legal discrimination and cultural stigma against lesbian, gay, bisexual, transgender and intersex (LGBTI) people and to recognising our equal citizenship and humanity.

Marriage brings with it many practical legal, financial, health and social benefits for same-sex couples and our families. Marriage equality will also strengthen the institution of marriage by allowing it to embrace those same-sex couples who want to uphold its values.

When we consider the purpose of marriage in today's society we can see that same-sex partners can fulfill that purpose. When we consider the objections to marriage equality we see they are not borne out by the overseas experience. When we consider the alternatives to marriage equality it becomes obvious there are no substitutes for the right to participate in such a universal and valued institution.

Finally, the urgent need for marriage equality, and growing support for reform in Australia and overseas, make a compelling case for decision-makers to act now.

In the process of addressing the benefits of marriage equality I touch on a wide range of issues from the stereotypes LGBTI Australians still endure, through the changes marriage has undergone, to the conservative case for marriage equality. But whatever case I make I anchor in the personal stories of same-sex partners and their families. Unless otherwise indicated, their words are from the 2009, 2012 and 2013 federal parliamentary inquiries into marriage equality.

1. Until they can marry, same-sex partners are not free and equal citizens

"Gay people, like all human beings, love and want to declare love, want inclusion in the community and the equal choices and possibilities that belong to us all... Marriage equality is the precondition for these rights, these protections, this inclusion, this full citizenship." [1]

US marriage equality advocate, Evan Wolfson

Equality and discrimination

For many same-sex partners and our family members the right to marry is about the equal recognition of our relationship in the law and in society, and the freedom to marry the person we love most in the world.

Shelley Argent, the national spokesperson for Parents and Friends of Lesbians and Gays, lives everyday with the stark reality of inequality. She has two sons, one gay and one straight.

"James came out at the age of 18, and though I'd made our home safe for him and although I felt no differently toward him, I was absolutely terrified of the uncertain future he faced in the outside world. I thought, 'This is not fair, his straight brother has the right to marry the person he loves'. They both started out with the same life but now, through this one admission, my son James would be prevented from living an equal life, not just by the attitudes of people but by outdated laws. I decided, as his mother, that this just wasn't

fair. He had done nothing wrong and it wasn't fair that he should be discriminated against in his own country." [2]

The principle Shelley highlights - that same-sex partners are not fully equal until they can marry - has been affirmed by courts and governments around the globe. In one of the ground-breaking court cases that led to marriage equality in Canada, the Supreme Court of British Columbia put it succinctly:

"...Redefinition of marriage to include same-sex couples...is the only road to true equality for same-sex couples." [3]

What is meant by "true equality" was brought into sharp focus in Australia in 2008 when the Federal Labor Government amended almost a hundred laws - governing everything from superannuation through taxation to social security and immigration - to ensure the spousal rights and responsibilities these laws grant flow equally to different and same-sex cohabiting or "de facto" partners. The single law from which discrimination against same-sex partners was not removed was the Marriage Act. As Davina Storer wrote in her submission to the 2009 Senate marriage equality inquiry (unless otherwise indicated, the ensuing personal stories are all taken from submissions to that inquiry and subsequent parliamentary inquiries[4]), the partial 2008 reform had the effect of highlighting that equality in marriage is the cornerstone of full legal equality:

"I applaud the changes made to many federal laws to acknowledge same sex entitlements. I believe it is fair that same sex couples are treated equally to everyone else and that we should all be taxed the same way. But this is only fair if same sex couples are treated equally in every way, not in a

watered down "partial equality" that suits the government, but still separates us from our heterosexual friends."

As Davina explains, equality does not come in half measures. It is particularly unfair to impose legal and financial responsibilities without corresponding legal rights. To borrow from America's founders, there should be no taxation without solemnisation. But there is also a deeper element to the idea of equality that is not limited to legal parity. Just as the meaning of marriage as an institution goes beyond the law to include social expectations and cultural norms, so too the "equality" in "marriage equality" takes in all the social and cultural discrimination, disadvantage and stigma a ban on same-sex marriage creates, reinforces or is used to justify.

Denying same-sex partners the right to marry sends out the message that our relationships are not equally worthy and valuable. It says we are not capable of the depth of love, commitment, joy and sacrifice associated with marriage. Impugning our love in this way is particularly damaging for lesbian, gay, bisexual, transgender and intersex (LGBTI) people because who we love defines so much about our lives, at least in the eyes of others. In the words of Jackson Tegg,

"It's hard to explain to people who aren't gay what it feels like knowing the law stops me from marrying. It's not what the law says I can't have that makes me feel excluded. It is what the law says I can't give"[5].

Discrimination in marriage also says it is acceptable to exclude an entire group of citizens from important social institutions on the basis of their sexual orientation. These

7

negative messages are magnified by the fact that marriage is the only federal law which still discriminates on the grounds of sexual orientation, and because marriage is such a central social institution.

An ever-growing body of social research shows the vulnerability of LGBTI people, particularly young people, to prejudice, stigma and discrimination. We can experience unacceptably high levels of discrimination in the workplace, discrimination in other aspects of our lives, including at school and in our families, and hate-motivated assault[6]. LGBTI Australians are also more likely to experience below-average health outcomes including higher levels of depression, due to this prejudice and discrimination[7].

Further, research confirms a direct link between these unacceptable levels of discrimination and exclusion from marriage. US studies have found laws preventing same-sex couples from marrying cause these couples to devalue their relationships, feel discriminated against, and experience high levels of stress and other mental health problems, regardless of whether the couples in question wish to marry[8] (for more on the link between discrimination in marriage and poorer health see chapter 3).

The largest study of Australian same-sex couples yet conducted, *Not So Private Lives* from the University of Queensland, has confirmed the American results[9]. It found the majority of same-sex partners believe their friends and family do not value their relationship as highly as marriage. According to the University of Queensland research, this perception of inferiority in the eyes of others is self-fulfilling in that it leads directly to poorer wellbeing and shorter relationships.

The direct link between exclusion from marriage, and anti-gay discrimination and stigma more broadly, should not come as a surprise. Exclusion from marriage keeps alive some of the oldest and most damaging misconceptions about same-sex relationships and LGBTI people. Thankfully, these misconceptions are slowly fading, which is partly why marriage equality became possible. But still they persist, making it necessary.

I've already touched on one such misconception: that same-sex relationships are unstable, unfulfilling and unenduring (for more on this see chapter 5). "You'll be unhappy and die alone", may no longer be the standard parental response to a young gay person coming out. But the myth is still sufficiently common to justify and satisfy the ban on same-sex marriages.

Another myth taking too long to die is that LGBTI people are a threat to the family, and particularly to children. Thankfully, the false conflation of homosexuality and paedophilia has now almost vanished from public debate. But discomfort about same-sex couples raising children, particularly if they are male couples, remains strong in some sections of society. As I explain in chapter 6, this discomfort has no basis in reality. Children in the care of same-sex couples are just as safe and happy as other children. But excluding same-sex couples from an institution seen by many as the proper legal foundation of family and child rearing allows old misconceptions to limp on.

Another old misconception, robbed of a timely death by the ban on same-sex marriage, is that same-sex attraction is an escapist whim, an act of rebellion, or the outgrowth of trauma, all of which can be healed by a combination of willpower, religious fervour and heterosexual marriage. From this misconception comes one of the most common responses to marriage equality from its critics: everyone already has that right to marry, as long as they do the right thing and marry someone of the other sex. The best science available says this is an unreasonable expectation because sexual orientation is deep-set and not easily malleable. Even organisations that once tried to convert homosexuals into heterosexuals, like Exodus International, have acknowledged this, apologised and closed shop. As the old "it's a lifestyle choice" myth evaporates, the "everyone can marry already" line is exposed as callous. It is also exposed as demeaning to the institution of marriage by promoting loveless unions that are, at best, extended therapy sessions.

Overt prejudice is not as strong as it once was, but there is still a sense among many LGBTI Australians that we are stigmatised. Take the practice, common in the Australian media, of only referring to an individual's homosexuality when they have done something wrong. If a gay man commits murder he will be headlined as "a gay murderer". If he wins a gold medal he will be a champion whose sexuality is considered irrelevant. The overall impression fostered by this double standard is that homosexuality is associated more with bad than good. As a result, homosexuals must work harder to win respect and risk more easily falling from grace. Many maligned minorities experience the same double standard, not least religious minorities like Catholics and Jews in early Twentieth Century Australia. Equality in marriage directly counteracts all these subtle but damaging ways LGBTI people are treated differently. It says the attitudes behind this different treatment are outdated, irrelevant and dying away.

The leading Australian intellectual to engage seriously with marriage equality, Raimond Gaita, grasps the link between legal discrimination and cultural denigration. For him, what lies behind marriage inequality is a lack of empathy, "a blindness to the full humanity of our fellow citizens".

"When gays ask to be granted the right to marry, they are not asking for something that can be adequately conceptualised by an ideal of equality that demands equal access to good and opportunities for all citizens of a polity. They ask, I believe, for the recognition, by their fellow citizens, of the depth and dignity of their sexuality; and they ask it from those of their fellow citizens who appear to believe that gay sexuality does not have the kind of depth that deserves to be celebrated in marriage. Married love, such people believe, deepens sexual love, but it can do so only for sexuality that has the potential for such deepening. They believe, therefore, that gay marriage is a kind of conceptual absurdity, even when they do not find it morally distasteful. There are many kinds of opposition to gay marriage: this kind has analogies with the incapacity of racists to see depth in the lives of the victims of their denigration."

In his submission to parliament about the impact of legal inequality on his life, Benjamin Bridge gives concrete expression to the link Gaita draws between discrimination in marriage and discrimination more broadly:

"Being officially and publicly denied the choice of whether or not I want to get married to the person I love has definitely had a negative impact on my life. I am unable to walk down the street as myself for fear of being discriminated against and heaven forbid I show public affection even if it were to just hold my partners hand. This kind of oppression permeates throughout every aspect of my life and affects how I work in my place of employment and even how I interact with my neighbours. Denying equal rights to all but some drives a rift into the subconscious of all Australians, creating an undesirable "us and them" frame of mind."

Marriage equality will not remove all anti-gay discrimination and stereotyping. But it will remove one of the last official refuges for prejudice. Neither will marriage equality erase the fact same-sex relationships have been persecuted and criminalised until very recently. But it will be the fastest-acting antidote to this poisonous past.

Freedom and citizenship

Alongside equality, personal autonomy, or the liberty to choose one's own marriage partner, has been identified by courts in other countries as a fundamental right breached by the failure to allow same-sex marriages.

According to the Massachusetts Supreme Court:

"Barred access to the protections, benefits, and obligations of civil marriage, a person who enters into an intimate, exclusive union with another of the same sex is arbitrarily deprived of membership in one of our community's most rewarding and cherished institutions. That exclusion is incompatible with the constitutional principle of respect for individual autonomy." [10]

The case for individual autonomy was frequently heard during the debate on decriminalising homosexual sex in Australia from the 1970s to the 1990s. It was not considered the role of the law, especially in a pluralistic, multi-cultural and multi-faith society, to impose the views of one section of society on everyone else. That outlook became less popular with the rise of gay identity politics. Acceptance of difference was demanded. It was no longer sufficient to tolerate. But toleration is indispensible when two sets of irreconcilable values collide. It is still important for each of us to respect the right of others to make their own decisions, especially in the private sphere, even if we don't agree with their choices.

Liberal Democrat Senator, David Leyonhjelm, has helped revive the "classic liberal" case for gay law reform and applied it to marriage equality. Speaking to his Freedom to Marry Bill in 2015 he likened the government telling LGBTI people who they can and can't marry to *"parents calling up a marriage broker and choosing their children's spouses for them"*.[11]

"I support marriage equality because I think people ought to have the freedom to choose their own life path. That is, they have liberty: as John Stuart Mill said, 'over his own body and mind, the individual is sovereign'. When the law says that gay, lesbian, bisexual, trans and intersex people cannot marry…the state is interfering, intervening, telling certain people that they can do what they want, except when they can't. I argue that while marriage may be part of the public sphere…it is a private choice."

Of course, there will be those who say allowing same-sex couples to marry is different to allowing consenting adults to have sex in private. They will say marriage is a public good that establishes norms and has an educative value whereas gay sex is private, victimless and has no public repercussions. But the gap is not really that wide. Leyonhjelm is right that the decision to marry is a private choice made for any number of personal reasons the state has no right to judge. At the same time, having one's sexual relationship punished, or not, by the criminal law has a wide variety of public repercussions. Respect for pluralism and toleration of difference apply equally to solemnising same-sex relationships as they did to decriminalising them.

We've seen already how the principle of equality goes beyond the law and includes removing social stigma. It is the same for the principle of individual freedom. For those people denied the right to marry the person they love, marriage is synonymous with freedom from second-class legal and social status.

The association between the freedom to marry and freedom from second-class status is well understood by those who have fought for the civil rights of people of colour.

In 1958, in the midst of the struggle for black civil rights in America, Martin Luther King Jr declared:

"When any society says that I cannot marry a certain person, that society has cut off a segment of my freedom." [12]

In 1959, the German-American philosopher and political theorist Hannah Arendt made the same point in greater detail:

"The right to marry whoever one wishes is an elementary human right compared to which 'the right to attend an

integrated school, the right to sit where one pleases on a bus, the right to go into any hotel or recreation area or place of amusement, regardless of one's skin color or race' are minor indeed. Even political rights, like the right to vote, and nearly all other rights enumerated in the (U.S.) Constitution, are secondary to the inalienable human rights to 'life, liberty and the pursuit of happiness' proclaimed in the Declaration of Independence, and to this category the right to home and marriage unquestionably belongs." [13]

Inspired by this idea, a black woman from Virginia, Mildred Loving, and her white husband, Richard, took state laws barring their interracial union all the way to the US Supreme Court and, in 1967, succeeded in having them struck down[14].

What many Australians don't know is that laws with an effect similar to those against which Mrs Loving fought, existed here for a century, and were central to the struggle for Aboriginal rights. Beginning in Victoria in the 1860s and reaching their most extreme form in Western Australia and Queensland in the 1930s, Aboriginal Protection Acts allowed state officials to determine who Aborigines could or could not marry. These laws were used for different purposes at different times. Queensland's policy was generally one of preventing black/white unions. WA's evolved in the opposite direction, preventing "half-castes" from marrying other Aborigines in order to "breed out the colour". But no matter what the racist purpose of these policies, the effect was the same: personal tragedy and political disenfranchisement[15] (for more on the Aboriginal struggle for freedom to marry, see chapter 14).

In 1935 the "half-caste" women of Broome had had enough. They declared in a petition:

"Sometimes we have the chance to marry a man of our own choice. We ask for our Freedom so that when the chance comes along we can rule our lives and make ourselves true and good citizens." [16]

Thanks to voices like these, freedom to marry rose to the top of the Australian Aboriginal rights agenda, second only to the right to vote, and stayed there until the states repealed their Protection Acts, and the national referendum of 1967 confirmed full Aboriginal citizenship.

Unlike most white Australians, Aboriginal Australians still recall the struggle for the freedom to marry, showing how critical it was to the emancipation of their people. For example, during the national human rights consultation in 2009, a member of the committee, Tammy Williams, responded to the issue of same-sex marriage by recalling how recently Aboriginal people had been denied freedom to marry.

"I couldn't help but think about my family, when you talked about the right to choose your partner ... In my family, it's only one generation ago that we were prevented from choosing our chosen partner to marry – not because of sexual orientation, but simply because of our race, our Aboriginality."

There is an obvious parallel between the historic struggle of blacks for marriage choice, and today's struggle by same-sex partners for the same choice. Mildred Loving understood this. On the 40th anniversary of the court decision that bears her name, she declared:

"I believe all Americans, no matter their race, no matter their sex, no matter their sexual orientation, should have that same freedom to marry." [17]

According to teacher, Kim Burman, her Australian Aboriginal students also grasp the link:

"When examining the case of Loving V. Virginia, one student pointed out the similarities between interracial marriage and same-sex marriage. She turned to me and said, "What's the big deal? Why does it matter who you love, or what you do at home? Why do they even care? When will they ever learn???" She was visibly upset and frustrated that her elders - the government, religious leaders, community members, those who she looked to for guidance - could not see the simple truth that she could."

Former President of the Australian Medical Association, Dr Kerryn Phelps, pulls no punches in her characterisation of the link between the freedom of interracial couples to marry and the freedom of same-sex couples to do the same:

"Today, most people can't imagine a situation where blacks and whites would still be banned from marriage. But some of us do not need to stretch our imaginations because we are living in a state of marriage apartheid... in Australia... right now... in 2011."

The link Phelps and others are drawing is not simply that blacks were once told which race to marry while LGBTI people are told which sex. It's not just that our respective relationships were considered undesirable or faulty, or bad for the children we have. It's not even, as Raimond Gaita argues, just about acknowledging that there is depth and value in our sexuality, as important as this is. As the Broome petition suggests, there is a direct link between freedom to marry and full citizenship.

Consider all the other groups in society, along with people of colour and LGBTI people, who at one time or another have been denied the freedom to marry the partner of their choice: women, people with disabilities, paupers and prisoners, servants and slaves, people from minority faiths, and people from different countries or ethnicities. What they all have in common is that they have been regarded as too immature or morally irresponsible to make what is arguably the most important decision any individual can ever make, the choice of a life-long partner. The reasons offered for denying each group freedom to marry was different: women were thought too irrational and sentimental to choose their marriage partners, while LGBTI people are stereotyped as perpetual teenagers unable to take on the responsibilities of marriage. But whatever the rationale, members of all the groups I listed have been told their hearts were untrustworthy and they should marry as society dictates, or not at all. In the same vein, the gradual acceptance that members of these groups are fully adult, fully citizens and fully human, has been accompanied by an acceptance of their right to marry whomever they wished (for more on the history of freedom to marry see chapter 14).

It is the acceptance of LGBTI Australians as fully members of the Australian nation and the human family which lies behind many people's support for marriage equality. My hope is for the day when, like Mildred Loving and the "half-caste" women of Broome, LGBTI people will be free to make our own choices and rule our own lives.

2. Being unable to marry creates legal disadvantages

I am an Australian citizen living in the United Kingdom who married an English person who is of the same sex. [But] the moment I stepped on to Australia soil (my home country!) my marriage was not recognised. My partner was hospitalised at St Vincent's and I was informed I had no more rights than a friend and could not be listed as her spouse on the paperwork hence was only allowed in during visiting hours.

Julianne Clark

Proof and portability

As partners who cannot marry, same-sex couples must meet a long list of prerequisites before they are deemed to have the legal rights granted to common law or "de facto" relationships. This usually includes a fixed period of living together. Partners who have recently met, who live apart because of work, or who have just moved from another state or nation can find it hard to qualify.

Even when partners do qualify as a cohabiting couple, their spousal status can be challenged by relatives and denied by the authorities. Going to court is often the only choice in such circumstances. This can involve great financial cost, the intrusiveness of testifying and being cross-examined about one's intimate life, and, of course, being publicly and irrevocably outed. As Julianne Clark reminds us, the failure to recognise a partner's rights can be particularly traumatic where one partner requires emergency medical treatment. But proving your spousal status can also be a problem in everything from superannuation entitlements to immigration. What's more, the need to establish the existence of a spousal relationship is more likely to arise for same-sex partners than for their different-sex counterparts. The idea that same-sex couples have legal rights is relatively new, and is still not understood or accepted by the relatives of some same-sex partners or by some hospitals, schools or workplaces.

One workplace that accepts the equal spousal rights of same-sex partners is the Australian military. But partners can only access spousal entitlements if they are married or can provide evidence of a long-term, financially-interdependent, cohabiting relationship beyond the level of evidence required to prove a civilian de facto relationship. Because service personnel in same-sex relationships cannot marry they have no choice but to provide this proof. The life-threatening situations some service personnel find themselves in makes this more urgent than for many civilians. But the common military experience of frequent deployments across the country and the world also makes it harder to meet requirements like cohabitation.

In the words of RAAF squadron leader, Vincent Chong, who has served in several deployments including in the middle east;

"When I received a short-notice posting to the USA, my partner and I had been in a committed relationship for around three years, but were not recognised by Defence. An opposite-sex couple in a similar situation elected to wed to receive family benefits. Had we been permitted to marry, we

would have done so to ensure that Defence looked after my partner during the overseas posting.

"When you are being deployed, worrying about whether your partner will be recognised and looked after by Defence is a distraction that you do not want to be dealing with, particularly when you are about to enter a life-or-death situation. History shows us that marriage registries tend to do a booming trade during wartime. The story of Australia's involvement in war cannot be told without telling the tales of soldiers marrying their sweethearts before leaving for the front line. Unfortunately, I cannot tell the same story. A marriage certificate is very simple, well understood and internationally recognised." *

Marriage equality eliminates all the legal uncertainty people like Julianne and Vincent experience by allowing couples immediate access to all spousal rights and protections, and guaranteeing these rights against all challenges. No doctor, bureaucrat, estranged parent or commanding officer can argue against a marriage certificate.

Another practical problem faced by same-sex couples because they can't marry is differences in the rights of de facto partners between the Australian states and territories. Some allow same-sex couples equal recognition as parents,

---

* The point about legal certainty for service personnel is underlined by the fact they are prepared to die for the very rights and freedoms they themselves are denied. Former soldier, Cameron Simpkins, made the point well when he vowed to "take up the sword" for marriage equality as a 2010 federal election Liberal Party candidate. He said, "I know a bloke who was in the SAS, who received the conspicuous service cross. He was a bloody good soldier. He was prepared to die for his country and protect our freedoms, and he can't marry the bloke he loves. To me that's just wrong."

others don't. The hurdles couples have to jump over to be deemed de factos also vary. In contrast, marriage provides the same rights and responsibilities wherever you live in Australia.

Davina Storer explains it this way:

"It might be hard to comprehend if you are not in a same-sex relationship, but we are often not even sure what our rights are a lot of the time, especially in different states. It is very sad, that in this day and age in Australia, the land of the 'fair go', there is still a group of citizens like us, who have to regularly log on to Google and devote significant chunks of time to working out what our rights are in different parts of Australia, whenever we embark on a normal couple milestone, such as moving interstate, buying a house, having children etc."

Inconsistency is even more of a problem between nations than it is between states. A marriage in one country is generally recognised in most others. Marriage is a legal contract that has "portability" as lawyers say. About sixty places overseas currently recognise same-sex marriages solemnised in other jurisdictions if we count internal states and provinces as well as entire nations[18]. Many of these places have large populations of Australian expats, and large expat populations in Australia. It is also sixty more than recognise Australian de facto relationships, and the number is growing all the time[19].

The fact that the list of nations allowing same-sex marriage is growing rapidly highlights another galling inequity: the Australian Government's failure to honour same-sex marriages solemnised overseas. When the Marriage Act was amended in 2004 to make it clear legally-recognised matrimony is limited to heterosexual couples, a provision was included explicitly banning the recognition of overseas same-sex marriages. Since then, several thousand Australian same-sex partners have married overseas[20]. Some of these partners are new Australians or expats like Julianne. Most go overseas specifically to marry, although they usually do so reluctantly. It is expensive, and an overseas marriage is far harder for families and friends to attend. If a same-sex marriage solemnised overseas breaks down, it can also be much harder and more expensive to obtain a divorce than it is for different-sex couples in Australia.

Some Australian states have stepped in to the breach, passing laws that recognise overseas same-sex marriages as state civil partnerships. First Tasmania, and now Queensland and NSW, automatically give same-sex couples married overseas the same spousal entitlements as married partners in state and federal law while still avoiding the "m" word. But this has created an entirely new set of problems. The UK recognises an Australian state civil partnership as the equivalent of a UK civil partnership. However, under UK law couples cannot be married and in a civil partnership. As a result, Australian couples who want to marry under UK law must first dissolve their Australian state civil partnership. In effect, they must choose between the dignity of marriage and the legal rights that come with not being married.

Given all the frustrations and absurdities created by the failure of Australia to recognise overseas same-sex marriages, no wonder the University of Queensland, *Not*

So Private Lives survey, found 91.3% of Australian same-sex couples married under foreign laws would prefer to marry in Australia[21].

But as Davina reminds us, for Australia's marriage refugees the right to marry is so profoundly important they are willing to make the sacrifice:

"My partner and I were recently married in Canada, but upon flying home to Australia, our marriage is not recognised and this has brought significant sadness to not only our lives, but to both of our families who were unable to travel to Vancouver to be with us on our special day. We spent a small fortune to be legally married. This was money we had been saving to put towards our first home deposit, but we made the decision to dip in to these funds to be married in a country where it was legally recognised and neither of us regret this for an instant."

Regret, no. But frustration, yes. In Julianne's case we saw the practical problems that arise when legal same-sex marriages are not honoured. But no less painful is the symbolism of having your matrimonial status stripped from you and your solemn vows count for nothing, the moment you walk back through Australian Customs. Davina again:

"By refusing to acknowledge our legally witnessed marriage overseas, you tell us we are not equal citizens in Australia. You tell us and the rest of the community that somehow our love and marriage is "less than" the rest of heterosexual Australian society. You make us feel unwelcome in our place of birth, compared to the compassion and understanding we receive in other countries that have true equality."

Transgender and intersex

The problems faced by transgender and intersex people too often go unnoticed in the marriage equality debate, as they do in society. But the fixation of Australia's Marriage Act on gender places particular legal burdens on them.

For example, in Australia a small number of married partners have undergone gender transition so they are now the same gender as their spouse. But if they seek to have their new gender recognised in identity documents like a birth certificate they must first divorce. Forced divorce where one partner is transgender is not actually a requirement of the federal Marriage Act. It is an overzealous demand of state laws put in place to uphold the exclusion of same-sex partners from marriage.

From the point of view of upholding the values of marriage, forced divorce makes no sense at all. It is absurd that a law made to defend marriage actually destroys some marriages, forcing some couples to break their vows of lifelong commitment against their will. It is equally wrong that those transgender partners who want to protect their marriage are forced to live a lie about their gender identity. Most of all, it is cruel that at a moment of stress in a relationship – the gender transition of one of the partners – the government wants to remove one of the partners' best buttresses, their marriage.

Listen carefully the next time you hear a politician talk about laws that force couples to divorce when one partner is transgender. If they defend forced divorce as a way to defend marriage they either have a highly abstract and ideological understanding of marriage far removed from the experience of most people, or their disdain for same-sex unions is so great they are willing to sacrifice existing marriages to satisfy it.

If the problem for transgender folk is that the law makes it hard for them to stay married, the problem for intersex people is that they can't marry in the first place.

Intersex people are born with anatomical and genetic characteristics of both sexes. Because the Marriage Act says only a man and a woman can marry, intersex people are excluded completely. Australian court decisions from the 1970s confirm this exclusion. There is a way around these rulings. Just as transgender people can lie about their true gender to stay married, so intersex people can hide who they are behind the old boy/girl divide in order to wed. But after struggling for a lifetime to understand and accept who they truly are, intersex people should not be expected to go back into the closet.

Australian intersex advocate, Gina Wilson, explains the painful choice the law presents:

"I have to confine myself to a lie to be entitled to marriage. I have to agree that I am either a male or a female and continue on with the shame and secrecy that has plagued me all my life. I have to hide that I am intersex, hide my actual physical characteristics of birth. My argument would be for a marriage equality bill before the parliament to allow intersex people to marry simply by making it a union between two consenting adults."

A good marriage is about what's in your heart, not what's between your legs. Yet the Australian Marriage Act says the opposite. The life stories of transgender and intersex Australians highlight this gap between what marriage is and what the law says it should be. Take just one story, that of transgender advocate, Martine Delaney:

"When I was still outwardly a man, I was married to a wonderful woman. She was a widow, with two sons who we raised together. Twelve years after we met – still married and very much in love - she drowned, moments after saving a young girl who'd been caught in a rip. I have since transitioned to being what I know I was always meant to be, a woman. I am again in a wonderful relationship with a woman I love very much and we are jointly raising my foster grand daughter. Yet, now I am not allowed to marry. I am still the same person. My current relationship is as committed and meaningful as my former marriage. Our responsibilities to each other, and to the child we look after, are the same. So why does the law treat us differently? Why could I marry then and not now? It makes no sense."

A wall of restrictions

Until recently, another way exclusion from marriage legally disadvantaged same-sex partners was the use of this exclusion to justify legal discrimination in areas of law and policy that go beyond who can and can't marry.

After it wrote a ban on same-sex marriage into Australia's Marriage Act in 2004, the Federal Coalition Government frequently used that ban to justify discrimination in other areas of relationship law. For example, it refused to recognise same-sex partners as de factos, even in uncontroversial areas like superannuation entitlements. State and territory civil union schemes providing same-sex couples with formal recognition and the entitlements of marriage were also targeted, especially in the Australian Capital Territory (ACT) that, constitutionally, is subordinate to the Federal Government.

Even in the complex regulations governing marriage, the ban on same-sex marriage initially had a long reach. It was used to justify rules banning registered celebrants from conducting unofficial same-sex commitment ceremonies (and from referring to different-sex partners as anything but "husband" and "wife" during their wedding ceremonies). It was the reason the government refused to issue Australian same-sex couples with the documents they require to marry overseas and which different-sex partners received as a matter of course (for more, see chapters 12 and 14). It was also the reason the government used for refusing to allow same-sex couples to marry under foreign laws in foreign consulates in Australia. For many years, whatever form of recognition they sought, and wherever they sought it, Australian same-sex couples could not escape the shadow of their exclusion from the Marriage Act.

In opposition, Labor supported the ban on same-sex marriage. When it won office in 2007 too little changed. As I've noted already, in 2008 the Federal Labor Government removed discrimination against same-sex de facto partners in areas like superannuation and taxation. It also allowed the ACT to adopt a civil union scheme which formally recognised same-sex couples, yet it still refused to allow couples an official, marriage-like ceremony. It maintained the Coalition's Government's refusal to allow foreign consulates to marry same-sex couples or issue same-sex partners with the documents required for them to marry overseas. Same-sex couples continued to be frustrated in their attempts to have official civil union ceremonies here, or official marriages under foreign laws.

As if it weren't enough to burden same-sex couples with the day-to-day legal problems that arose from being unable to marry, successive Australian Governments used a single discriminatory law – the Marriage Act – as the foundation for a wall of policies and regulations to defend the definition of marriage from local and global change (for more about the restrictions built around the 2004 Marriage Act amendment, and what ideas lay behind them, see chapter 14).

Fortunately, this has begun to change. In what amounts to a slow retreat from the 2004 amendments, many of the restrictions on same-sex equality mentioned above have since been lifted. After the 2011 Labor Party national conference adopted a pro-marriage equality policy, the ban on same-sex partners receiving the official documents required for overseas same-sex marriages was removed. In the same year Tasmania allowed partners entering civil unions to have officially-recognised ceremonies. Today, civil celebrants are less often harried for officiating at same-sex relationship ceremonies or told how to refer to marrying partners, although they are still warned not to use the words "wedding" or "marriage" to refer to same-sex ceremonies. None of the old restrictions have been re-imposed by the current Coalition Government, despite Prime Minister Tony Abbott's opposition to marriage equality. Indeed, when the UK asked permission to marry same-sex couples in its Australian consulates in 2013, the Coalition Government agreed, effectively lifting the ban on same-sex couples marrying in foreign consulates. Since then over 100 couples have married in Australia's UK consulates[22].

As the wall of secondary restrictions have been chipped away, the primary restriction – on same-sex couples marrying under Australian law – has come to look increasingly out-of-step. But the legacy of all these petty regulations persists, both in uncertainty about what regulations currently apply and the fear they could always return as long as marriage inequality persists.

3. There are health and financial benefits to same-sex couples, their families and society

"Marriage remains an economic bulwark. Single people...are economically vulnerable, and much more likely to fall into the arms of the welfare state. Furthermore, they call sooner upon public support when they need care—and, indeed, are likelier to fall ill (married people, the numbers show, are not only happier but considerably healthier)."

The Economist on the need for marriage equality,
January 1996[23]

Health

As I noted in chapter 1, same-sex attracted people suffer worse health outcomes because of discrimination and stigma, particularly in the area of mental health. Psychologists call it "minority stress". A number of studies have found a direct relationship between poorer health outcomes and exclusion from marriage. This has prompted respected mental health organisations like the American Psychological Association (APA), the Australian Psychological Society (APS) and Australian youth mental health advocates, Headspace, to issue statements in favour of marriage equality[24].

Dr Damien Riggs from the APS reminds us when a group is excluded from key institutions society as a whole is affected:

"Marriage discrimination has a flow-on effect on same-sex attracted Australians, their loved ones, and the wider community. Psychologists must work to ensure that all Australians are supported to achieve positive mental health and full social inclusion."[25]

Headspace considers the impact on future generations:

"Marriage equality is primarily about ending social exclusion and giving all Australians the same basic rights. Lack of equality has strong links to mental health issues among same-sex attracted young people. We want to see an end to the unnecessary stigma and isolation another generation of young Australians could face because of this inequality." [26]

To grasp how exclusion from marriage and mental health are linked in the daily experience of LGBTI Australians, consider this case study from Queensland psychologist Paul Martin:

"A mother came in with her seventeen year old son who she found just in time, as he had made an attempt on his life. He was an intelligent, caring, much-loved son, brother and was well regarded at school. I asked him 'why'. He said that when he was at school being a fag was the worst thing to be called, that his Dad had talked negatively about 'poofters'. When he realized he was gay he struggled with depression due to fear of rejection and a sense that he was worthless and his future was without hope. He started watching 'It Gets Better' videos on YouTube and began to feel that he may in fact be able to live a good life. But then, just before he was about to come out to his parents, he saw the Prime Minister, Julia Gillard, on TV saying that marriage is between a man and a woman and she would not be supporting marriage equality, without giving any real reasons. At that moment he realised that everything he'd ever been taught about what it means to be gay was in fact true, that he wouldn't be able to live a good life with a long term partner and happy future. This for him was the tipping point where he chose to end his life."

Just as marriage discrimination has a measurable negative impact on health, so marriage equality has a demonstrable positive impact. In their review of the studies into the health of same-sex couples who marry, Yale Law Professor William Eskridge, and his colleague, Darren Spedale, identified specific health benefits for these couples, including the lower levels of stress associated with being more open with family and work colleagues and even lower levels of HIV and other STDs[27]. The most recent, and largest scale, US study of same-sex married couples corroborated these conclusions. It found that,

"Same-sex married lesbian, gay and bisexual persons were significantly less distressed than lesbian, gay and bisexual persons not in a legally-recognised relationship." [28]

The positive health impacts of marriage equality aren't limited to removing discrimination. There is also a health dividend from marriage generally. A growing body of research shows that regardless of gender, married partners are, on average, healthier, happier and longer lived than their cohabiting peers, or singles[29]. In the words of the APA,

"Marriage bestows substantial psychosocial and health benefits to individuals, due to the moral, economic, and social support to married couples." [30]

According to the US Centre for Disease Control, even rates of heart disease, drug use and stress are lower among married partners.

As you would expect, these general health benefits of marriage flow on to same-sex partners who are married. A 2011 study of lesbian couples in Massachusetts confirmed this:

"Results support the finding in the heterosexual marriage literature that a healthy marriage is associated with distinct wellbeing benefits for lesbian couples." [31]

A study from the University of Ottawa into the impact of marriage on the health of Canadian same-sex couples came to a similar conclusion.

"...the participants indicated that marriage had an overwhelmingly positive impact on their lives." [32]

Clearly, marriage equality has a positive impact on the health of same-sex couples and their families. What's more, it has this impact twice: once through the removal of legal discrimination and again through the benefits of marriage. The same goes for the financial benefits of marriage equality.

Money

The most commonly-heard financial argument for marriage equality is that the national economy will benefit from the wedding spend of same-sex couples. Independent research from places with marriage equality shows local economies have gained from same-sex couples spending money on their weddings. In turn, this spending generates much-needed employment, while some goes back to government in the form of tax revenue and marriage licence fees. What's more, much of this money is "new spend" that would not otherwise be available to the economy. For example, same-sex couples spent $259 million in New York City in the first year of marriage equality, with $16 million going directly to the city government[33]. It has been estimated that the overall economic impact of marriage equality across the US will be about $2.6 billion, including $185 million in state revenues. This will create over 13,000 jobs[34].

Based on the international experience we can fairly confidently estimate how much the Australian economy will benefit from same-sex weddings. We take the number of same-sex couples recorded in the last Census (33,700, which is a significant under-estimate of the actual number according to the Bureau of Statistics[35]), multiply that by the percentage who say they will marry if they can (53% according to the *Not So Private Lives* study) and multiply that again by the average wedding spend of Australian heterosexual couples (estimated to be at least $36,200, although some estimates put it at almost $50,000[36]). The result using these figures is at least $646.5 million.

The simple formula I have used was developed by the acknowledged experts in this field, the Williams Institute at UCLA. But they use more conservative figures in their calculations. Because same-sex couples may have previously celebrated their commitment in an unofficial ceremony, may not have the financial support of their parents, or may have their incomes reduced by the pink ceiling, the Institute assumes same-sex wedding spend to be a quarter of the average. Its estimate of same-sex wedding spend in Australia is $161 million. This bare minimum is still a sizable amount, and we should add to it the spend on receptions and honeymoons, as well as the spend of those foreign same-sex couples who come to Australia to wed.

But whatever the final amount could be, we can be certain it is being eroded by Australia's failure to enact marriage equality. Thousands of same-sex partners have already married overseas. Thousands more will follow, if their home country refuses to treat them fairly. Money that could have been spent in Australia, creating jobs for Australians, is instead boosting the economies of foreign countries, all because of prejudice and politics.

The economic impact of marriage equality does not end with wedding spend. LGBTI tourists are more likely to travel to countries where they are treated equally. Skilled migrants in same-sex marriages are more likely to settle in countries that treat their marriages with equal respect. Heterosexual members of the so-called "creative class" are increasingly likely to see marriage equality as a sign that a society is tolerant and forward-thinking. When faced with two countries with similar economic fundamentals, investors will look to issues like marriage equality to distinguish which country embraces change, looks outward and values personal freedom. Last but not least, workplaces are more productive when all staff feel equally respected and protected.

In 2015 Australia slipped out of the Lonely Planet and Huffington Post's lists of top gay travel destinations for the first time since the lists began. Our place was taken by countries like Iceland, Scotland and Uruguay. All have marriage equality. The president of Gay and Lesbian Tourism Australia, Rod Stringer, doesn't believe this is a coincidence:

"...the move by an increasing number of nations to legalize same-sex marriage is influencing travel choice. Sadly,

Australia is viewed as one of the least progressive in this regard and that is not helping to attract international visitors."[37]

When he was a Senator for Western Australia, Brian Greig also saw the negative economic impact of marriage discrimination first hand. Here he outlines the cases of two foreign men with much-needed medical skills who wanted to migrate to Australia:

"(There was) a desperate need in parts of rural and regional Australia for qualified psychologists and psychiatrists. Many country hospitals had long-standing vacancies and an urgent need for top quality counsellors. Problems arose when, by coincidence, two unrelated gay men from Britain answered the call and made plans to come here to offer their skills, expertise and training to regional communities. Despite both men being in separate long-term relationships, the Commonwealth refused to recognise these gay couples as 'family', meaning that they would enter Australia as legal strangers to their respective partners. It also meant that the immigration procedure was more complex, frustrating and, frankly, offensive. If, in the event they did come here, only one partner in each relationship (the one filling the medical job) could work whilst here. Their spouses were not permitted to do so. This employment prohibition does not apply to heterosexual spouses. Both couples were taken aback by this revelation. Both were shocked to discover that the relaxed, tolerant and 'fair go for all' Australia they had believed in was a myth. In the end both doctors and their respective partners went to New Zealand which did not discriminate."[38]

An even bigger issue for business is the impact of government discrimination in the workplace. In the business sector it is now commonly accepted that workplaces are more efficient and productive when staff feel their contribution is valued and there are no barriers to their participation. For this reason the Diversity Council of Australia, a not-for-profit business advisory group on workplace diversity, has endorsed marriage equality:

"There is much to be gained in terms of reputation, recruitment, retention, productivity and market share from ensuring that workplaces are welcoming and inclusive of employees and customers, irrespective of sexual orientation, gender identity or intersex status. Marriage equality will truly cement workplace fairness and inclusion for the LGBTI community." [39]

Partner in Allens law firm, Rachel Nicholson, agrees. For her, marriage equality is all about treating a staff member as "a whole person" rather than expecting them to leave an important part of themselves at home.

"The fewer barriers there are to being able to function effectively as a whole person in the workplace, the more productive you are and that has a knock-on effect from an economic perspective." [40]

Given the economic impact of marriage equality it's no surprise the reform has the support of a wide range of Australian businesses, including all four major banks and both major airlines. In the words of former head of the Australian Industry Council, Heather Ridout:

"I don't think the issue of gay marriage could be described as a radical, left-wing agenda....it's very relevant to many Australians." [41]

But there is another economic impact of marriage equality that goes beyond the private sector and beyond the initial post-reform economic bounce. It centres on the link between marriage, personal finances and government expenditure.

Research shows that the failure of governments to allow same-sex couples to marry limits their financial self-reliance and heightens their risk of welfare dependence.

After reviewing this research, British academic, Michele Calandrino, concluded:

"Since same-sex partnerships are not legally recognised, homosexual people do not have the possibility to form their own legally protected family. [Legally recognized] families... represent strong safety nets for individual workers and this possibility of "income-insurance" is not open to homosexuals."[42]

In the Australian context this is less of a problem now the financial and workplace entitlements of same-sex de facto partners have been legally recognised. But, insofar as married partners are more financially interdependent and more likely to stay together longer, including at times of personal crisis, the economic safety net marriage provides different-sex partners is missing for same-sex partners. Calandrino and others have identified the economic consequences of this absence – for both same-sex partners and society. They include a) a disincentive to maximize earning, savings and investments, to plan or take any of the financial risks necessary to increase personal capital, b) a heightened risk of falling into the welfare net, and c) a reduced capacity to engage in wealth creation.

As research fellow at the Institute for Public Affairs, Chris Berg, has argued,

"Marriage is a private form of social welfare. Spouses insure each other against sudden loss of income. Married couples are less vulnerable to financial stress than single people. Extending the marital franchise to gay and lesbian couples would multiply the number of Australians who can join this crucial social institution, spreading the positive impact of marriage on society." [43]

Amanda Vanstone, a former minister in the Howard Government, also acknowledges the importance of marriage equality for promoting financial reliance between partners and lessening reliance on the state.

"The…point I would make to conservatives – if you believe as I do you should try and look after yourself, be independent and be an individual, then you are going to have to do that with others. You're going to have to have relationships and admit dependence on other people. That's what people do when they get married. They say 'We are going to be dependent on each other'. I think conservatives should welcome more people openly saying 'I'm going to have a life relationship with this person, we will be dependent on each other, we are going to ask things of each other instead of asking from the State'. I think conservatives should welcome more recognition of interdependence." [44]

"For richer for poorer, in sickness and in health": clearly there are benefits to be had from making these vows, benefits which are blind to our sexuality and gender. For ordinary Australians like Allan Swanepoel it makes no sense to value the benefits of marriage but then hesitate to extend them to same-sex couples:

"I have a gay son, I have always loved him and always will, regardless of his sexual orientation. I feel that for him not to have the fruits of marriage, like I have for the last 30 years, simply goes against all democratic and basic fundamentals of life."

4. There are social and cultural benefits to same-sex couples, their families and society

"I have been in a happy relationship for 38 years. My partner and I were both migrants arriving to Australia in the '50s. We were a controversial pair. He was German and I was Jewish who not so long before spent my childhood and adolescence in a concentration camp. Yet we overcame a great obstacle because we have found love was stronger than hate. We built our lives, together. We brought family to Australia, who in turn prospered and had families of their own. We lived in the same house we bought and had a wonderful relationship with our neighbours and people at large. Our foundation was solid. We did not shake any heterosexual foundations.

"We would have loved to be married and be part of society instead of outsiders. I think that in a more enlightened world there should be more understanding and tolerance for persons of the same sex to be allowed to marry and live equal as heterosexuals. With the staggering number of divorces around me I wonder how much stronger our foundation was by comparison."

Frederick Weisinger

Marriage provides partners, families and the general community with a universal language for love, commitment and relationships. Terms like "husband", "wife" and "wedding" are immediately understood. Marriage is also one of the universal legal and social institutions through which we find connection and a sense of belonging, not only with our partner, but with our families and communities.

An example of this social aspect of marriage is the fact marriage conventionally creates kinship between families as well as partners, hence terms such as "mother-in-law" and "brother-in-law". Marriages are usually solemnised by a representative of the state, not only between the marrying partners, but in the presence of family members and friends. Traditionally, those present at a wedding are symbolically involved in the ceremony by being asked to voice their view on the union "or forever hold their peace".

This is just one of the many traditions associated with marriage. They vary from wearing your grandparent's wedding ring and having your parents walk you down the aisle to carrying "something old, something new, something borrowed and something blue", tying tin cans to car bumpers, or joining in the bridal waltz. Such traditions persist because they allow family members and friends to affirm the new union and bind the new couple to existing family and social structures. They allow us to feel connected to generations past, present and future. Of course, these traditions have no legal standing and can be included in ceremonies not recognised by the law. But they are given added depth and meaning when associated with the binding legal vows made during a marriage ceremony. They also have great significance for LGBTI people, given how often we have been ostracised from the lives of our birth families, how callously we have been stigmatised as "anti-family", and how hard we have fought to reclaim a sense of belonging.

Another example of the social function filled by marriage is that it is commonly regarded as a rite of passage. As well as being a way to increase our connection with family, marriage has traditionally (and paradoxically) been seen as the moment young people leave their parents' household and found a new one. This is less so today, but marriage is still seen as an important step in establishing greater independence from our family of birth. News reports of the deaths of Sydney siege victims, Katrina Dawson and Tori Johnson, showed how strong this perception still is. Dawson and Johnson had been with their respective partners for about the same time. But only Dawson was able to marry. As a result, references to Dawson's next of kin always cited her husband and children first. References to Johnson's nearest and dearest almost always cited his parents first, and only then his partner, Thomas Zinn. Insofar as marriage opens the door to adulthood, those banned from marriage are infantalised.

Allowing same-sex couples to marry includes us in the pervasive language, rites and traditions associated with marriage, many of which are fundamental to everyday interaction. This provides same-sex partners with a sense of participation and belonging not otherwise available. Former Tasmanian Social Inclusion Commissioner, David Adams, explained this when he was lobbying for Tasmanian law-makers to support marriage equality in 2012.

"Marriage remains an important bridge between inclusion and exclusion for many people. It can represent increased commitment to spouses and bring increased feelings of acceptance by family and community. Children of same-sex parents feel happier having married parents and feel more secure and protected. Parents of same-sex people feel happier and more included in their community when their children can marry."

"Marriage as an official union is important in that it is a form of social license to act in day-to-day ways most of us take for granted. For example: to be the primary family visitor in a hospital where our spouse is a patient; to show affection; to go house hunting together; or to be in family photos. Similarly, from the perspective of family and community members the status of marriage provides an endorsement to relate openly and freely, and not feel concerned by being labelled by association."

Research backs up the very real social and cultural benefits David Adams points to. A landmark study led by Lee Badgett, Professor of Economics at the University of Massachusetts and research director of the Williams Institute describes and quantifies some of these benefits in two different places that have allowed same-sex marriages for over a decade, the Netherlands and Massachusetts[45].

Professor Badgett found same-sex partners overwhelmingly:

- marry for the same reasons as different-sex couples, chiefly because of their shared love and commitment

- felt marriage had increased their commitment and their sense of responsibility, and had generally strengthened their relationships

- believed their children were better off after their marriage, chiefly through legal protection for those children and enhanced feelings of security, stability and acceptance in the children, and

- felt participation and acceptance in their extended families and communities had increased because of their marriage

Her conclusion was that:

"Overall, the experiences of same-sex couples in two countries, the United States and the Netherlands, suggests that same-sex couples and their families are strengthened by a policy of marriage equality for same-sex couples."

Dr Darren Cundy and his partner Warrick concur:

"Marriage is to us a cross-generational ceremony that provides a framework and context for families to come together to offer their support and blessing. Marriage 'says' to a couple, your family acknowledges you, your community acknowledges you and the law of the land acknowledges you. To preclude a couple from marriage on the basis of sexuality sends just the opposite message."

At a time of growing social isolation, exclusion and alienation, when many people yearn to find a genuine connection with others, it seems perverse that we continue to exclude same-sex couples and their families from such a universal and fundamental institution of social connection as marriage. As much as anyone, LGBTI people understand the harm caused by this exclusion. It is no coincidence that, in the quote opening this chapter, Frederick Weisinger directly linked exclusion from marriage to exclusion from society. As his story reminds us, marriage is about building bridges not barriers. By allowing same-sex couples to marry, Australia will have affirmed, not only that discrimination is wrong, but that same-sex couples belong, and that, for everyone, marriage is still where we find one of our deepest and most fulfilling connection with others.

5. Marriage equality is good for marriage

"The fact that not everyone in Australia can marry actually made me hesitate to get married earlier this year. I felt that if I got married with the law the way it is, I would be supporting the current marriage laws that disallow same sex couples recognition."

Marie Brown [46]

Strengthening marriage

The debate on same-sex marriage often focuses on the benefits of equality for same-sex partners and their families, but there are also benefits for marriage as a legal and cultural institution.

Allowing same-sex couples to marry will admit many more couples who seek to uphold the core values of marriage and are enthusiastic for the institution. It will send out the message that marriage is defined by love and respect, not prejudice and discrimination. It will also prompt different-sex couples to re-value wedlock as an institution in which the over-arching values are love, devotion, and not least, connection. It shows everyone that marriage is relevant and resilient enough to embrace changing social attitudes.

The Times of London expressed this succinctly when it endorsed marriage equality in 2012.

"Far from damaging marriage, expanding it to same-sex couples shores it up. Stable gay relationships are part of

national life. If marital law cannot accommodate them, the purpose of marriage will eventually be brought into question." [47]

Melbourne-based pro-equality Baptist pastor, Rev. Nathan Nettleton, goes even further, arguing that the future of same-sex unions and marriage generally are inextricably linked.

"Heterosexual marriage is under threat, but the threat is from within and not from without. The real threats to marriage come from the commodification of sex and relationships and a consumerist mindset that sees everything as ephemera that can be discarded and replaced as soon as a new model comes along that offers a greater level of satisfaction. Unfortunately, when things that we hold dear are under threat from things we feel powerless to tackle, we have a tendency to deflect the blame onto a scapegoat. I think that is what the churches have often tended to do with the homosexual community. But now what we have here is a group who are recognising the value of marriage—of faithful, lifelong vowed relationships—and asking for the right to participate in the benefits of that. Surely if a group who have been stereotyped as the champions of hedonistic promiscuity begin extolling the virtues of marriage, that can only increase the regard in which marriage is held by the community as a whole."

Evidence that allowing same-sex marriage uplifts marriage can be found in those places where the recognition of same-sex relationships has a relatively long history. In Scandinavia, the formal recognition of same-sex relationships has been in place for longer than anywhere else in the world, and same-sex marriage is now widely allowed. At the same time, marriage rates among heterosexual couples have increased after decades of decline; divorce rates have stopped increasing, as has the number of children raised by unmarried couples[48]. Similarly, those US states that allow same-sex couples full marriage rights have the lowest rates of divorce among heterosexual partners. The state which has had marriage equality the longest, Massachusetts, has the lowest divorce rate of all[49], while those states that banned same-sex marriage have the highest divorce rates[50]. A review of these examples, published in *The Wall Street Journal* in 2006, agrees none of this is a coincidence:

"There is no evidence that allowing same-sex couples to marry weakens the institution. If anything, the numbers indicate the opposite" [51].

The research has grown so compelling it has persuaded many social conservatives to support marriage equality. In 2015 a number of prominent US Republicans and conservatives led by retired four star general, Stanley McChrystal, submitted a brief in support of marriage equality to the US Supreme Court. It read in part,

"...the facts and evidence show that permitting civil marriage for same sex couples will enhance the institution, protect children, and benefit society generally. Banning marriage for same-sex couples, in contrast, undermines these critical societal goals. Such bans impede family formation, harm children, and discourage fidelity, responsibility, and stability."

The signatories concluded that *"...marriage is strengthened, and its value to society and to individual families and couples is promoted, by providing access to civil marriage for all American couples—heterosexual or gay or lesbian alike."* [52]

American writer, Jessica Shortall, gives this argument a human face. While attending a gay community fundraiser she was inspired to value her relationship with her husband even more than she had.

"As someone who was born straight, marriage was always just laid out in front of me, ripe for the taking whenever I wanted.... It was never something I had to fight for, to dream about, to yearn for. The people in that room Saturday night treat marriage like a priceless treasure. That doesn't mean they don't have bad days or months or years, or don't fight over who is doing bedtime, but it is one hell of a good reminder for every marriage. So you LGBT advocates can stop saying that same-sex marriage won't affect my marriage, because it will. In fact, it has already made my own marriage better." [53]

Will marriage be destroyed or demeaned?

Opponents of marriage equality argue exactly the opposite, declaring that same-sex marriage will variously "demean", "degrade" or "destroy" the institution of marriage. There are even individual heterosexual couples, usually conservative Christians, who claim there will be a negative impact on their own marriages. They are the religious right's answer to same-sex couples telling their personal story about the impact of inequality. But how their wedding vows will be diminished by other couples taking similar vows is often hard for them to explain except by an appeal to abstractions. Heterosexual couples who believe their love and commitment will be shaken by the actions of complete strangers show an amazing lack of confidence in themselves and the institution they say they champion.

As for marriage as an institution, let's take a look at the claim same-sex marriages will "destroy marriage". My disputant when this book was first published, Bill Muehlenberg, argued that heterosexual marriage, is a "universal", "bedrock" institution so fundamental to society that allowing two men or two women to marry would not only "effectively destroy" marriage[54] but put our "continuity as a culture in jeopardy". Science refutes this one-sided view of the history of marriage. Anthropologists have found that in many different cultures – from medieval China and Japan to pre-modern Africa, America and Polynesia - same-sex relationships have been regarded with respect and sometimes treated as marriages, albeit almost always those between men[55]. As the Yale history professor, John Boswell, argued in *Same-Sex Unions in Pre-Modern Europe*, the Catholic Church itself recognised same-sex unions right up to the end of the Middle Ages, developing liturgies specifically for such ceremonies[56]. Clearly, the exclusion of same-sex couples from marriage is not "universal", and marriage-like relationships between same-sex partners are an important part of history. For that reason, and to counter the misinformation of people like Bill Muehlenberg, the American Anthropological Society issued the following statement in 2004.

"The results of more than a century of anthropological research on households, kinship relationships, and families, across cultures and through time, provide no support whatsoever for the view that either civilization or viable social orders depend upon marriage as an exclusively heterosexual institution. Rather, anthropological research supports the conclusion that a vast array of family types,

including families built upon same-sex partnerships, can contribute to stable and humane societies." [57]

Respect and recognition for marriage-like same-sex relationships has a history as long as marriage itself. But even if, for the sake of argument, marriage has always been an exclusively heterosexual institution, this doesn't mean it should continue to be. In modern times we have slowly but steadily shaped a society in which women are legally and socially equal to men. There are few, if any, other societies in history which have aimed for or achieved this goal. Opponents of equal rights for women frequently pointed this out, claiming human society can only survive when men are in charge. They were wrong. Bill Muehlenberg's opposition to same-sex couples marrying falls into the same category. He justifies an old exclusion by nothing more than the fact it is old.

Those opponents of marriage equality who claim marriage will be demeaned and diminished, generally consider same-sex relationships shorter, less stable, sinful and/or entirely sexual. I will deal with sin in the next chapter. For now let's consider the claim same-sex relationships are less loving and less committed than different-sex counterparts, and hence less marriage-like. To back up this view, opponents of marriage equality often cite studies that show gay men are highly promiscuous. Beware of such studies. They often compare, for example, married different-sex couples with unmarried same-sex couples including those who wouldn't marry even if they could[58]. They draw their samples from inner-city bars, clinics and sex clubs because their focus is on gay men at high HIV risk[59]. Many of these studies go out of their way to exclude men in monogamous relationships because they are not at risk. A good example is a Dutch study of HIV risk among young, inner-urban gay men commonly miscited by the Australian Christian Lobby to show gay male relationships only last an average of eighteen months[60].

The selective use of statistics by opponents of marriage equality is matched by their equally selective deployment of quotes from gay men who either aren't looking for committed relationships, or are explaining to a sometimes hypocritical world why gay men who have multiple partners, while not necessarily more common, may be more honest about it. In the same way ordinary, committed same-sex partners living in the suburbs are less likely to show up in studies, they are less likely to make an appearance in commentary, literature and pop culture. They don't match the gay stereotypes audiences like to be titillated or horrified by.

But they are, nonetheless, what this debate is all about. Statistics purporting to show gay men sleep around are not only misleading and unrepresentative, they are also irrelevant. When it comes to whether same-sex partners are capable of the commitment associated with marriage, we should be looking at those partners who already value commitment, not those who eschew it, because it will be the former who are likely to marry.

In contrast to the isolated and misconstrued studies and examples cited by groups like the ACL, there is a substantial body of peer-reviewed research which indicates many same-sex attracted people form committed relationships that are long term, and these relationships have the same qualities as different-sex relationships[61]. A large scale study of same-sex couples registered under the Vermont's civil union scheme found virtually no difference between same-sex and different-sex couples. In its words,

"what's most interesting about this analysis…is the banality of the results. Civil union households simply don't differ that much from those of the general population" [62].

A subsequent study released by the University of Minnesota confirmed this result. It found that the LGBTI people surveyed valued romantic love, faithfulness and commitment no less than their heterosexual peers. One of the largest studies ever of same-sex partners, conducted at Stanford University in 2014, found no difference between the longevity and stability of same and different-sex relationships[63]. But perhaps the most important evidence of all comes from those nations that allow same-sex marriage. When we compare divorce rates between same-sex and different-sex couples in the Netherlands, since same-sex partners were permitted to marry in that country in 2001, we find they are exactly the same[64]. A recent report comparing divorce rates in two US states shows same-sex couples are less likely to divorce than their different-sex counterparts[65]. Clearly, same-sex couples are just as capable of the level of commitment associated with marriage as their heterosexual peers. Seen from this perspective, marriage equality is simply about the recognition in law of those many same-sex couples who are already married in fact.

The opponents of marriage equality couldn't be more wrong when they declare same-sex relationships lack the marriage-like qualities to be found in different-sex relationships. But for the sake of argument, let's suppose same-sex relationships are more unstable and uncommitted. Isn't this an argument for same-sex marriage rather than against it? Opponents of marriage equality clearly believe homosexual promiscuity is a bad thing. They clearly believe marriage is a way to promote values like commitment. They should be some of Australia's strongest advocates for marriage equality. The fact they aren't suggests they have a fundamental belief, which they simply use statistics to bolster, that same-sex relationships are beyond redemption; as well as a fear, odd in people who believe so ardently in marriage, that the institution is too weak to lift same-sex couples up[63].

As well as believing marriage is too feeble to positively influence same-sex relationships, marriage equality opponents fear it is such a fragile institution any change poses a risk too great to take. But if we look at the history of marriage we can see it is a highly adaptable and resilient institution that has changed immensely over the years, and that these changes, far from weakening the institution, have strengthened it.

It is only in relatively recent times that partners married for love. Before that, marriage was primarily about the inheritance of property, shoring up ethnic or religious identity and, as we will see in the next chapter, the begetting of children. This is why fathers arranged their children's marriages and women lost all their legal rights upon marriage. It is why rape was allowed within marriage but contraception banned. It is why interracial unions were barred and inter-faith unions frowned upon. As old ideas about the purpose of marriage changed, so did the laws governing it. Divorce was allowed so partners could escape abusive or unhappy marriages, equal rights were extended to unmarried de facto partners and their children, marital rape was prohibited, wives were given legal equality, and, as already mentioned, barriers to interracial marriages were removed. When each of these changes occurred, opponents of change claimed the institution of marriage would be demeaned, diminished or destroyed. Clearly, this was not the case. Instead marriage was reformed, renovated and rejuvenated so that it remained relevant in an ever more tolerant and egalitarian age. Same-sex marriage is part of the same tradition of reform and renovation.

The real threat to marriage

Citing examples of how marriage has changed reminds us not only that these changes were inevitable but that change is essential for marriage to survive. Imagine if marriage was the same institution today that it was a hundred years ago when wives were virtually property, divorce nearly impossible and the races effectively segregated? It would no longer be considered relevant and few heterosexual couples would wish to marry. The same consideration applies to same-sex marriage. As society becomes more accepting of same-sex relationships, the current prohibition on same-sex marriages will come to be seen as anachronistic, and the institution of marriage as a whole will be increasingly seen as an instrument of prejudice rather than a symbol of love.

Journalist Matthew d'Ancona understands the dangers of marriage becoming a relic, and recruits GK Chesterton to make the point that things only stay the same when we allow them to change:

"I am grateful to Ian Ker's magisterial new biography of GK Chesterton for the following observation by its subject: 'All conservatism goes upon the assumption that if you leave a thing alone, you'll leave a thing as it is. But you do not. If you leave a thing to itself, you are leaving it to wild and violent changes.' ... Chesterton was scarcely a moderniser. But his point applies well to the institution of marriage. In an age of impatience, lives based on tactics not strategy, and instant gratification, matrimony is in dire need of renewal and restoration. ... If marriage is indeed the cornerstone of a stable society then its extension to same-sex couples will be a stabilising force. Gay couples who marry will not only be exercising a new right; they will be recruited to, and reinforcing, an ancient institution." [67]

The real threat to marriage today comes not from those same-sex couples who seek to become part of the institution and uphold its values, but from those who would make marriage a vehicle for their prejudices, and who would fossilise the institution until it is as repellent and irrelevant as these prejudices are fast becoming.

We can already see this happening in Australia. In my experience, an increasing number of heterosexual partners share the view of Marie Brown, whose words opened this chapter, that marriage is diminished by the discrimination against same-sex relationships that is entrenched in the Marriage Act. Some even go so far as to refuse to marry while their gay and lesbian friends can't. A high profile example is Australian rugby player, David Pocock, and his fiancée, Emma Palandri, who had a ceremony in 2011 but refused to sign the official marriage papers until all Australians have the same right[68].

In the ears of more and more Australians, the words celebrants are obliged to say at all marriage ceremonies - "under Australian law marriage is the union of a man and a woman *to the exclusion of all others*" - risks becoming a declaration of prejudice rather than an affirmation of fidelity. But there is hope. It is offered by those countries that have proven same-sex marriage enhances marriage and society rather than diminishing them.

Like every Australian marriage refugee, Davina Storer has seen this with her own eyes:

"During our time spent in Canada, the country seemed to be functioning well, and there was no evidence that having same-sex marriage has destroyed family values or broken down social functions in any way. The religious institution of marriage is alive and well there and has not been destroyed, and life goes on as usual, and Canadians can truly say that they have equality in their country."

6. Religion and children are arguments for marriage equality, not against it

"My husband David and I married in a Quaker ceremony in Canberra 2007. The irony of being able to have a religious ceremony but being prevented from achieving legal recognition due to arguments about the 'sanctity' of marriage has always struck me as highlighting one of the many absurdities in the continuing discrimination against gay, lesbian, bisexual and transgender people. "

Evan Gallagher

The Bible and procreation are the two most common arguments against marriage equality. For some people marriage is a holy sacrament and same-sex relationships sinful. We can assume this is what the former head of the Australian Christian Lobby, Jim Wallace, was getting at when he wrote several years ago that the "personal faith" of some senior politicians was the reason for their opposition to same-sex marriage[69]. For others, same-sex couples are incapable of reproducing while the whole purpose of marriage is to have children. This is why former Prime Minister, John Howard, said banning same-sex nuptials was justified on the basis that "same-sex marriage does not contribute to the survival of the species"[70].

Religion

Some people of faith say their religion determines that a marriage can only be between a man and a woman. For some of these people heterosexual marriage is a holy sacrament. For some it is part of God's plan for the world as shown by the Bible or derived from the Natural Law He set in place. For still others, marriage, like any virtue in a sinful world, is easily corrupted by non-believers. For most, marriage is incompatible with same-sex relationships because such relationships are inherently disordered and sinful.

My own conversations with evangelical friends and family members reveal deep-seated and conflicting assumptions about marriage and homosexuality. For them marriage is founded on sacrifice: not just day-to-day sacrifices for the good of one's partner and family, but the forsaking of one's fundamental desires and aspirations in order to follow God. Homosexuality is seen as the direct opposite of sacrifice. It is an indulgence, an expression of excessive lust, an idolatry of the self, by an otherwise heterosexual person. From this perspective, marriage and homosexuality are not just incompatible, they are inimical and irreconcilable.

These assumptions are being questioned like never before. Within some moderate Christian, Jewish and Buddhist communities this questioning has been occurring for decades. It has led to the appointment of openly-gay clergy and to the celebration of same-sex unions. What is changing now, suddenly and rapidly, is that questions are being asked within traditionally more rigid denominations. In the Catholic Church, Pope Francis has begun a church-wide dialogue on welcoming LGBTI people and acknowledging the value of our relationships. In the Pentecostal church, leading pastors like Australia's Brian Houston, have done the same.

This shift is in response to high levels of support for same-sex marriage among younger church-goers, the greater visibility of same-sex couples and their families in church congregations and the reinterpretation by theologians of Biblical passages once thought to condemn homosexuality. The upshot is that ever more faith leaders are distinguishing between those same-sex unions where traditional Christian family values like fidelity, mutuality and sacrifice are lived out and those where they are not. More traditional churches have not yet reached the point where they embrace marriage equality. But at least it is now possible they one day may.*

As welcome as these changes are, we must never forget the distinction between marriage as a civil institution and marriage as a religious rite. In the past there was a clear separation between these two different forms of matrimony. Marriage pre-exists all modern religions, including Christianity. Early Christians married under Roman civil law and did not observe marriage as a sacrament. Only in the Middle Ages did marriage as a civil institution and marriage as a religious sacrament converge[72].

In modern times, religious and civil marriage have again diverged. In Australian law, and before that, in the British legal system Australia inherited, there has been a clear

---

* One indication of changing religious attitudes to marriage is the decision by traditionalist churches, including the conservative Anglican archdiocese of Sydney, to allow atheists, Muslims and other non-Christians to marry in Anglican services[71]. The church's double standard of allowing non-Christians to marry in religious services while resisting the marriage of same-sex couples in civil ceremonies undermines the religious case against marriage equality.

distinction between civil and religious marriage. The Australian Marriage Act does not refer to the marriage codes of any faith, Christian or otherwise, except insofar as it allows religious ministers to solemnise legal marriages. It is because of this distinction that Australian marriage law a) allows divorce, even though some faiths expressly prohibited it; b) prohibits polygamy, arranged marriages, child betrothal and the subordination of married women, even though these are commonly found in the Old Testament; and c) allows marriage between people of different faiths or no faith. It is inconceivable that we would question the right of atheists to marry because they are considered ungodly by some people of faith. To bar same-sex partners from marriage for the same reason is a double standard.

The legal distinction between civil and religious marriage reflects the same distinction in society. According to the Australian Bureau of Statistics (ABS) 71.9% of marriages in 2012 were performed by a civil celebrant rather than a minister of religion. This compares to 42.2% in 1989[73].

The distinction between civil and religious marriage is clear, even to many of those who believe strongly in the latter. Australian Catholic lawyer, John Heard, is among those who believe there is no threat to religious marriage from allowing same-sex couples to marry:

"For many years I wrote in defence of the traditional and religious definition of marriage. I spoke to and wrote for conservative and religious audiences in Australia and overseas. There came a time, however, when I realised that the thing I was describing, this idea of traditional and religious

marriage that I believed was (and still believe is) worth defending, was not at all at risk from reforming the Marriage Act. *Civil marriage is an institution deliberately removed from the sacramental economy of the Christian Church. Civil marriage eschews the beliefs of any religious body. Parliament can reform the* Marriage Act, *then, to allow for same-sex civil marriage and, if the changes are handled correctly, the reform can have no effect whatsoever on religious marriage in Australia.*

"After many long years of argument, it is clear that I primarily objected to changes to the Marriage Act *because the changes discussed do not accord with my religious beliefs. However, civil marriage per se, divorce and so on do not accord with the same. I subscribe to the non-religious test model of democracy. I support freedom of religion. If one believes there must be civil marriage…it is unfair not to extend it to same-sex couples. The non-theological argument many social conservatives and religious people try to run against same-sex civil marriage is really an argument against civil marriage per se. It is also, by extension, an argument against marriage in any religion or tradition distinct from one's own. In a nation with no established church or religion such arguments are legally moot."* [74]

Rather than appeal directly to their religious belief, some religious folk invoke human rights in their case against marriage equality. They declare same-sex marriage will impinge their freedom of religion because they will be forced, against their beliefs, to conduct marriage ceremonies for same-sex partners. What they ignore is that in no country that allows same-sex marriage has this occurred. They also ignore the fact that in Australia religious marriage celebrants are not forced to marry anyone against their will (for more on this see chapter 7).

However, freedom of religion *is* a real issue for those Christian denominations that conduct same-sex marriage ceremonies in their churches but are denied the same governmental recognition of these marriages that other churches receive for the heterosexual marriages they solemnise.

In explaining his support for marriage equality, Rev Nathan Nettleton, argues:

"the doctrine of separation of church and state, for which some of my Baptist forebears endured violent persecution, teaches us firstly that it is a Christian duty to defend the right of others to follow their own conscience before God, free from coercive attempts to impose conformity of belief or practice; and secondly that the state should not privilege the convictions of any particular religious tradition, even a majority tradition, over the convictions of those who dissent from it."

Put simply, while Biblical injunctions against homosexuality are not a clear-cut or legitimate argument against marriage equality, religious freedom is a compelling argument in favour of it.

Children

A similar case can be made about procreation. We do not demand from marrying different-sex partners that they intend to have children, or impose any such legal requirement on them. This is why we allow partners to marry if they are infertile or past childbearing age, and to stay married if they use contraception, don't have sex, don't want children, or for whatever reason don't reproduce. It is also why Australian law provides the same legal rights, protections and responsibilities to unmarried parents and their children. In the words of retired Uniting Church minister, Rev John McRae, "marriage is no longer legal permission to have children"[75].

Again, this legal regime reflects changing social norms. According to the ABS, the proportion of Australian children born outside marriage is increasing, while the proportion of heterosexual couples with children, compared to those without children, is declining[76].

But there is still a widespread belief that marriage benefits children by providing them with stability and security, which brings us to the other side of the argument: an increasing number of same-sex couples are raising children - approximately 10-20% according to most studies[77], a figure which rises to almost 50% of female partners over 36 according to a recent national study[78]. By any count, this is many thousands of Australian children.

The Australian Christian Lobby thinks this is a bad thing, and another reason to oppose marriage equality:

"Children benefit most from having two biological parents of the opposite sex. They need the love and role models of the different genders that a mother and a father can provide, and they need this ideal of marriage to aspire to. Any redefinition of marriage risks deliberately placing children in relational constraints which deny them a mother or a father." [79]

Some marriage equality critics have taken this point even further, arguing same-sex parenting is comparable to forced adoption and the stolen generation of

Aboriginal children. According to David van Gend from the Australian Marriage Forum, just as Australian parliaments have apologised for forced adoption, so they will eventually apologise for allowing same-sex parenting when evidence of the damage it causes becomes overwhelming[80]. Meanwhile, the Australian Christian Lobby accused Prime Minister Kevin Rudd, whose legacy includes an apology to the Stolen Generation, of creating another stolen generation when he came out in support of marriage equality in May 2013[81]. This earnt a strong rebuke from Pastor Ray Minniecon, head of the Kinchela Boys Home Aboriginal Corporation and himself a member of the Indigenous Stolen Generation:

"The assimilation policy of forced removal of children from there homes and the subsequent abuse of those children is no way comparable to the desire of a loving couple to have a child and have their relationship recognized." [82]

The real perversity in this argument against marriage equality is that the prejudices behind the forced abduction and adoption of children in decades past – that entire groups of people make bad parents and particular types of families are better than others – are of a kind with prejudices that lay behind the condemnation of same-sex marriage and parenting today.

So how does science respond to these prejudices? Studies from Australia and overseas show children in the care of two parents of the same sex are not disadvantaged by being raised by these parents. One of the best summaries of the research on same-sex parenting was put together by the Australian Psychological Society in 2007. It found that

"...parenting practices and children's outcomes in families parented by lesbian and gay parents are likely to be at least as favourable as those in families of heterosexual parents, despite the reality that considerable legal discrimination and inequity remain significant challenges for these families." [83]

Reinforcing the message are the following statements from the American Pediatrics Association and the American Academy of Child and Adolescent Psychiatry, respectively.

"Research comparing children raised by homosexual parents to children raised by heterosexual parents has found no developmental differences in intelligence, psychological adjustment, social adjustment, or peer popularity between them." [84]

"Outcome studies of children raised by parents with a homosexual or bisexual orientation, when compared to heterosexual parents, show no greater degree of instability in the parental relationship or developmental dysfunction in children. There is no basis on which to assume that a parental homosexual orientation will increase likelihood of or induce a homosexual orientation in the child." [85]

The American Psychological Association (APA) goes one step further, addressing common criticisms of same-sex parenting studies by opponents of marriage equality: they have small sample sizes, don't use control groups and don't look at how children turn out as adults. The APA notes,

"The relevance of this criticism has been greatly reduced as research has expanded to explore life in a wider array of lesbian mother and gay father families...and as newer studies begin to include a wider array of control groups. Contemporary

research on children of lesbian and gay parents involves a wider array of research designs (and hence, control groups) than did earlier studies. "[86]

Significantly, the APA highlights the single study – by Australian researcher, Sotirios Sarantakos - upon which many marriage equality opponents have based their offensive claim that children suffer from same-sex parenting.

The APA says,

"the anomalous results reported by this study--which contradict the accumulated body of research findings in this field--are attributable to idiosyncrasies in its sample and methodologies and are therefore not reliable" [87].

In contrast, an Australian study published in 2014 by Dr Simon Crouch – the largest and most robust of its kind ever conducted in the world – found children of same-sex parents not only do as well as their peers, they actually "enjoy better levels of health and wellbeing than their peers from traditional family units"[88].

Not surprisingly, groups like the Australian Christian Lobby remain unconvinced. In 2011 the ACL commissioned Professor Patrick Parkinson to report on the environments in which children thrive. He concluded children do best when raised by their married, biological parents[89]. This was seized upon by opponents of marriage equality to argue the reform is a "recipe for social collapse" and a "crazy [attempt] at social engineering and thought control"[90]. But this is not what Parkinson's evidence showed, nor is it what Parkinson himself later admitted he meant[91]. The evidence his report cited found children do best when they are raised continuously by the same parents and their family life is stable. For most children this means being raised by their married, biological parents. But, of course, for children born to same-sex couples it means being raised by the only parents they have ever known and for these parents to be able to marry. Research that was meant to show the benefits of "traditional marriage" actually showed the benefits of extending marriage to same-sex couples[92].

The same problem in a more extreme form arose with the much-publicised parenting research of Texan academic, Mark Regnerus, published in 2012. He compared children raised continuously by their married, biological, heterosexual parents with children from "broken homes" where one parent was involved, however briefly, in a same-sex relationship. Regnerus concluded parental homosexuality was the reason for the poorer outcomes of the latter group of children, when it was actually family instability. Regnerus' research, if it is to be taken seriously at all, is, like Parkinson's, an argument for marriage equality not against[93].

But let's assume all this is wrong. Let's assume the children of same-sex parents do strike problems, particularly because of the prejudices of others. Surely one of the best ways to improve the lives of the children being raised by same-sex couples is to provide them with the legal protection, emotional stability and social legitimacy that comes with having married parents. Again, we strike the contradiction at the heart of the argument against marriage equality: if there are problems associated with same-sex parenting this is an argument in favour of marriage equality, not against.

The benefits to same-sex couples and their children of both marriage and the right to marry were noted earlier in chapters 1, 2 and 3. They include legal security, the removal of harmful discrimination, and a stronger sense of stability and connection. As Elizabeth Murray confirms, the only deficiency associated with same-sex parents is the law's failure to acknowledge their love:

"I lived with my mum and her same sex partner from the age of 10. I could not have had a better set of parents. They are my role models when it comes to how a long term relationship should look, and I hope my husband and I are as happy as they when we have been together for 20 years. Yet these women, who I love dearly, are denied the opportunity to legally marry. They came to my wedding and celebrated with me - yet I cannot celebrate the same happy occasion with them. Their union is like a marriage in every sense, so why are they denied that legitimacy? Why was I denied the legitimacy of my parents being married?"

While the capacity to conceive is not and should not be a pre-requisite for marriage, the stability and acknowledgment marriage brings benefits the children of straight and gay couples alike.

Our other half

An argument often associated with the procreational case against marriage equality, is that marriage is about the complementarity of the sexes. In other words, men and women are essentially different in a way that makes their union somehow more meaningful.

The newspaper columnist Piers Akerman believes:

"Among humans, marriage is the joining of a man and a woman, different sexes, one whole....At the simplest, a marriage is reflected in the relationship between a nut and bolt. A single nut is not much use. Neither is a bolt, but the two used in tandem as they are designed to be used, form an effective fastener. Two nuts don't make it, nor two bolts. Try to put them together and they don't marry." [94]

If Akerman is making an argument about penises and vaginas he is demeaning marriage. A good marriage is about much more than the configuration of one's reproductive organs. As we've seen, the value for children of having married parents lies in the stability and continuity that can bring, not in what genitals their parents have and what they do with them.

If Akerman's argument is about differences between men and women more broadly then his stance is profoundly sexist. It assumes gender is a more important feature of an individual than his or her character, abilities or morality. This is an argument thinkers have taken issue with for centuries. In *The Symposium* Plato reminds us that gender is irrelevant when it comes to finding our "other half":

"And so, when a person meets the half that is his very own, whatever his orientation, whether it's to men or not, then something wonderful happens: the two are struck from their senses by love, by a sense of belonging to one another, and by desire, and they don't want to be separated from one another, not even for a moment." [95]

As we've seen, the chief preoccupation of marriage equality opponents is to define marriage as something which precludes same-sex couples, chiefly with appeals to what God wants, what children need, and what gender difference demands. Even among opponents of marriage equality who reject the idea that same-sex relationships are somehow inferior, there are many who believe there is some inherent difference between same-sex and different-sex unions which makes the former unable to fulfill the requirements of marriage as they have defined it. Then Federal Opposition leader, Tony Abbott, expressed it this way:

"I am not against gay people having solid lasting relationships. I just don't think these can be called "marriages" any more than a rose could be called a gardenia or vice versa notwithstanding that they're both beautiful and sweet scented." [96]

Is this inherent incompatibility between same-sex relationships and marriage real or just rhetorical? It's clear from both the law and prevailing social attitudes that the purpose of civil marriage in modern Australia is not to discharge a religious duty, or procreate, or "fasten" the sexes. So what is its purpose, and can same-sex couples fulfill this purpose?

I believe most Australians today would agree the role of civil marriage is no more and no less than to legally entitle and socially acknowledge a loving, committed, enduring, romantic relationship. I also believe a majority would agree that same-sex relationships can be as loving, and as deserving of legal protection, as their different-sex counterparts. This is why, with overwhelming public support, the equal marriage-like characteristics of same-sex relationships have been established as principles of public policy in Australia through the recognition of same-sex de facto marriages at every level and in every area of law.

Australians today no longer believe same-sex relationships are intrinsically different, or unfit for marriage. Through familiarity with LGBTI friends and relatives, heterosexual Australians have come to understand that sexual orientation does not determine our desire for, or experience of, love and commitment. They understand, often far better than their leaders, that wherever love blooms into a life-long union, a single vine, our common humanity, gives it bud.

7. There will be no unintended consequences

"We come in peace."

Former convener of Australian Marriage Equality
Alex Greenwich

In chapters 4 and 5 we looked at the argument from opponents of marriage equality that the institution of marriage will be diminished by allowing same-sex couples to wed because same-sex and different-sex relationships are fundamentally different and the former are not marriage-like. This argument is a direct challenge to the case for legal equality I make in chapter 1. When two things are unequal in fact it is harder to argue they should be equal in law. But what we saw when we looked at the evidence is that there is an equivalence between same and different-sex relationships when it comes to love, commitment, child rearing and other customary elements of marriage.

Now, let's turn to the challenge opponents of marriage equality issue to the case I made in chapter 1 for personal freedom. Freedom can only be allowed if it does not impinge on the freedom of others and does not damage society. To make their case against the freedom of LGBTI people to marry, opponents of reform argue this freedom threatens their freedom of religion and expression, and will launch Australia down a slippery slope to polygamous marriages. Fortunately, there is one advantage to Australia being on the rapidly diminishing list of western countries yet to achieve marriage equality: we can see that such dire predictions about the "unintended consequences" of marriage equality have not come true.

Violating religious freedom

Of great concern to some religious opponents of marriage equality is that allowing same-sex marriages will lead to the violation of religious freedom. In particular, they say religious marriage celebrants and civil celebrants with a religious faith will be forced to marry same-sex partners against their beliefs, religious welfare agencies will be forced to violate their tenets by acknowledging same-sex married partners, business owners with a religious faith will be forced to be involved in same-sex weddings, and schools will be forced to teach that same-sex marriages are acceptable against their values or the values of individual parents. The alarm is particularly loud from the Australian Christian Lobby (ACL):

"Are Australians happy for fellow citizens who believe in man-woman marriage to be sued in the courts or driven from their jobs because of their beliefs, as is now happening in other jurisdictions?" [97]

When closely examined, the overseas examples cited to back up these concerns are often dubious or irrelevant. For example, in its submission to the 2014 Senate inquiry into the recognition of overseas same-sex marriages, the ACL cited several examples where it believes religious freedoms have been violated. However, most of these examples were from places without marriage equality[98]. The "violations" in question actually arose from appeals made under laws against discrimination and had nothing at all to do with same-sex marriages. The ACL's examples of religious freedom being "violated" in Australia fall into the same category. They are about appeals made under anti-discrimination laws and don't involve marriages at all. A typical example is a court decision against a Christian youth camp in Victoria for refusing to hire facilities to a gay youth group. The ACL has been too quick to blame marriage equality for things that are not its fault.

Same-sex couples can marry in twenty-one countries across five continents with a combined population of over 800 million people, yet in all these countries the ACL can only find a tiny number of what it alleges are examples of religious persecution. Let's look at the two most commonly cited examples. The first is from the US where marriage equality and religious freedom are more contentious issues than elsewhere. It is alleged that marriage equality in Massachusetts violated the religious freedom of the parents of school students by leading to same-sex marriage being "taught" in the class room. However, this claim has been repudiated by Massachusetts' public education officials who have pointed out their curriculum is set by lengthy consultation processes involving parents, and not by legislators[99], just as it is in Australia. The second example is from Denmark where, it is alleged, the Danish Government has "forced" church ministers to marry same-sex couples[100]. What opponents of marriage equality fail to acknowledge is that the ministers concerned belong to the established state Lutheran church under the direct control of government and are state employees. This is not comparable to the Australian situation. They have also failed to acknowledge that a Danish Lutheran minister can refuse to marry a same-sex couple as long as they find another who will. Even with these two headline examples, it is hard to see a direct link between marriage equality and so-called religious persecution.

More often, examples of religious freedom being violated are not examples at all, but simply unlikely extrapolations. A good example is an article by the vice president of the Australian National Civic Council, Patrick Byrne[101]. It melded a UK lawsuit that is unlikely to succeed, community advocacy against anti-discrimination exemptions, and the above-cited Danish example, in an unconvincing attempt to show Australian churches will be forced to marry same-sex couples. What people like Byrne consistently fail to acknowledge is that the Marriage Act already contains a provision allowing religious marriage celebrants to refuse to marry anyone at all. Not only will this section continue to apply once same-sex couples are allowed to marry, it will be strengthened by another provision specifically and explicitly exempting religious celebrants from marrying same-sex couples.

As for civil celebrants, and faith-based welfare agencies, schools and businesses, like everyone else the delivery of their services are covered by federal, state and territory anti-discrimination laws. Every Australian jurisdiction has its own detailed and well-considered legislation regarding discrimination on the grounds of sex, sexual orientation and gender identity. Each provides greater or fewer exemptions for religious conscience and practice. Apart from the ACL, Australian religious organisations seem satisfied that these laws currently provide sufficient protection for their religious freedoms. They aren't demanding broader exemptions to deal with unmarried or divorced different-sex couples, unmarried same-sex couples, single parent families, or people of different faiths and no faith. So why do they fear their legal protections will prove useless when same-sex couples are able to marry? In the same vein, faith-based welfare agencies and schools have established administrative policies on how they deal with unmarried or divorced different-sex partners and unmarried same-sex partners. Why can't these simply be expanded to include same-sex married partners? If existing laws don't provide sufficient protection for religious freedom, why don't faith-based schools and businesses just apply for an exemption, as is their right? This would be preferable to punching a giant hole in anti-discrimination laws that may inadvertently allow all manner of prejudice through.

I have heard some supporters of marriage equality harshly address concerns about religious freedom. They say religious people who claim marriage equality will violate their freedoms are cynically using the reform as cover to roll back existing anti-discrimination laws, or are easily misled by priests and pastors whipping up groundless fears to keep a grip on their congregations. There is also a perception some Christians are so keen to follow Jesus to martyrdom, as proof of their piety and righteousness, they will exaggerate, invent or invite persecution. This narrative draws on research showing the persecution of the early church by pagan Roman authorities "was almost entirely an invention" of secure and powerful church leaders writing centuries later[102]. Some historians claim that even when writing about the "Great Persecution" under Emperor Diocletian, church polemicists like Eusebius were "able to take a few instances and make you think that's what was happening everywhere"[103].

New Testament professor, Candida Moss, herself a person of faith, has written compellingly about the myth of persecution both in ancient and modern times. She has described the temptation to buy in to it, as well as its disastrous consequences for human empathy and democratic debate.

"Members of any Christian group can claim to be persecuted as long as they feel opposed. The cultural power that drives these claims…is the idea that Christians have always been persecuted. In Christian terms, if you're being persecuted, you must be doing something right."

"A defensive insensitivity that refuses to acknowledge the sufferings of those with whom we disagree is far too often where this obsession with persecution leads….In a world filled with persecution, efforts to negotiate or even reason with one's persecutors are interpreted as collaboration and moral compromise. We should not attempt to understand the other party, because to do so would be to cede ground to injustice and hatred….Framed by the myth that we (Christians) are persecuted, dialogue is not only impossible, it is undesirable….The myth of Christian martyrdom and persecution needs to be corrected, because it has left us with a dangerous legacy that poisons the well of public discourse." [104]

These views may be compelling for some progressive Christians and for non-believers, but they do not help assuage what are often the genuinely-felt concerns of many people of faith. They may make it harder. Instead, we must always refer back to the overseas experience, particularly in countries that are like Australia. Rev Margaret Mayman is a Uniting Church minister who has lived and worked in both New Zealand and Australia. Few people are as well placed to assess the religious impact of marriage equality:

"Marriage equality in New Zealand has not diminished religious freedom. In fact it has been enhanced. Prior to the legislation being passed LGBTI-affirming churches were unable to act according to their faith by legally marrying same-sex couples. Now they have that choice. Religious celebrants whose understanding of marriage does not extend to same sex couples are still free to choose not to marry same-sex couples if they wish. Marriage equality is not a threat to religious freedom. It is a spurious argument that is not borne out by the experience of churches in countries that have marriage equality."

Like many other people of faith Margaret does not believe marriage equality is a threat to religious freedom. In her eyes it is more about fear than fact and should not be allowed to cloud the key issues.

"Pink-tinged tyranny"

Closely associated to the fear that marriage equality will violate religious freedom is the fear it will violate freedom more broadly.

The most articulate exponent of this view is the atheist libertarian, Brendan O'Neill, who has labelled marriage equality "the death of freedom" and "the final act in a pink-tinged tyranny". His primary concern is that

"Allowing the state to redefine ancient, organic relationships is a short step from allowing it to police them. The political thirst for gay marriage is underpinned by officialdom's instinct to get a foot in the door of the family." [105]

In O'Neill's rhetoric there are echoes of those southern US whites who defended racial segregation in the 1960s. Pro-segregation Alabama Governor, George Wallace, accused President Kennedy of "power thirst" when the latter sent in troops to desegregate southern schools. Wallace urged his fellow southerners to "rise to the call of the freedom-loving blood that is in us and send our answer to the tyranny that clanks its chains upon the South"[106]. But, as with American firebrands like Wallace, O'Neill's fears about change are not borne out by reality.

O'Neill cites the Canadian government's decision to have marriage and birth certificates refer to "spouse" and "parent" rather than "husband", "wife", "mother" and "father"[107]. But this removal of gender from official forms is not contingent on marriage equality. In fact, it is already occurring in Australia even though we do not have the reform. This is because it is part of a much broader historical movement – gender equality. O'Neill's disdain for "spouse" and "parent" is equally a disdain for "chairperson" instead of "chairman" and "police officer" instead of "policeman". In the same way, his case against the state "redefining ancient, organic relationships" is also a case against the state legislating to remove the age-old "right" of a husband to have sex with his wife against her will.

By blaming gender-neutral terms on marriage equality O'Neill also fails to grasp that many same-sex partners want to marry precisely so they can be part of a traditional institution and call themselves "husband" or "wife". O'Neill should take comfort in that fact. But, like so many opponents of marriage equality, he seems unable to grasp that the reform he fears actually flatters the institution he values.

Perhaps knowing historical perspective weakens his case, O'Neill resorts to twisting the facts. For example, he writes damningly about "the spilt blood of French protesters and the trampled-upon right to dissent of Americans..."[108]. The American reference is to Brendan Eich, the former CEO of internet company, Mozilla, who stood down after it was revealed he had donated to an anti-marriage equality campaign. The problem was less the cause he donated to than the fact his job description required him to be above political controversy and to bring Mozilla's diverse clientele together, not polarise them. The French reference is to a protest against marriage equality in Paris that degenerated into a riot. After anti-marriage equality rioters pelted police with stones, bottles, flares and fireworks, police responded with tear gas[109]. This episode reflects on those who oppose marriage equality, and possibly the passion of French protesters, but not on marriage equality itself. It also reflects on O'Neill that he thinks there is a defensible freedom to throw incendiary devices, but not to marry the one you love[110].

As with alleged violations of freedom of religion following marriage equality, allegations of authoritarianism by marriage equality supporters are too often taken out of context, or are actually about something other than marriage equality. When we stand back from these red herrings, we see that those countries with marriage equality are, by and large, some of the freest in the world by any of the standard measures of individual autonomy, protection against government abuses and respect for human rights. Countries that persecute people for participating in or even talking about same-sex marriages – Uganda, Egypt,

Russia - are some of the least free and most corrupt. This should be no surprise. As we've seen in previous chapters, marriage equality is both a product of, and contributor to, the store of human freedom.

Freedom from fear

Those people who speak loudest about tyrannous, freedom-hating marriage equality advocates are mute about those who suffer for supporting marriage equality. This includes harassment and threats aimed at community advocates and members of the public who publicly support the reform. It includes vilification and threats of violent death against politicians who move the issue forward in parliament[111]. It also extends to loss of employment. In 2011, Melbourne Baptist minister, Rev Matt Glover, was sacked from his church roles for supporting marriage equality[112]. Sydney Baptist minister, Rev Mike Hercock, had a similar experience after he expressed support for marriage equality with the backing of his congregation. In 2013, just before Christmas, he lost his job and the house that went with it. He and his wife had to scramble to find new accommodation for their young family. Rev Hercock's congregation was also punished, losing its church building.

The religious hierarchs responsible for this persecution argue church ministers knew the rules when they signed up for the job. But this is hard to accept when the religious leaders in question make such sweeping claims about their own freedoms being violated. Glover and Hercock were moved to support marriage equality by their religious consciences. In Hercock's words, "there is no higher principle for Christians than walking in the shoes of others and treating them as we would wish ourselves to be treated". They are part of a denomination – the Baptists - with a long history of dissenting from established state churches, of being persecuted for this dissent, and of allowing its congregations unusual independence. Despite their support for same-sex civil marriage, Glover and Hercock both made it very clear they would not defy church policy by marrying same-sex couples in church ceremonies. It was reasonable for them to expect their opinions on marriage equality would be respected.

I have received a great deal of hate mail and several death threats because of my marriage equality advocacy. Up until now I have been reluctant to talk about this publicly. I don't want to encourage further threats. Unlike some opponents of marriage equality, I have no desire to associate all those who disagree with me with the bad behaviour of the tiny, abusive minority. Most of all, I want my arguments to win support on their merits, not from sympathy for me. I break my rule here in defence of people like Glover and Hercock. Like them, I have been blamed for the harassment I have received. Too often I have been told I should expect mistreatment when advocating on controversial issues. I have never agreed. It should be possible to participate in public debates without threats to one's livelihood or life. I also break my rule to highlight just how contrived the complaints of opponents of marriage equality can be. They cry foul when they are described as "bigots" or "homophobes". Yes, the use of these words is often unfair. Many people opposed to marriage equality do not harbor prejudices. But still, to call this "religious persecution" or "suppression of free speech", as the Australian Christian Lobby often does, is hyperbolic nonsense when we consider what some Australian marriage equality supporters have endured, not to mention what many Christians in other countries suffer.

When opponents of marriage equality accept that supporters of reform have freedom of conscience, freedom of religion, freedom of speech and freedom from fear – freedoms that are as valid as their own, and much more often violated – the sincerity of their own claim on these freedoms will be less open to question. Until then, their cry of "religious persecution" looks like a deliberate distraction from the fact they are defending discrimination.

A slippery slope to polygamy

The most commonly cited "unintended consequence" of marriage equality is that it will lead society down a slippery slope to the legitimisation of any number of unacceptable, unconventional or non-marriage-like relationships.

The extreme case is that allowing same-sex partners to marry will lead other people to demand the right to marry their dogs, cars and plasma screens. When Senator Cory Bernardi suggested same-sex marriage would legitimise sex with animals many people laughed it off [113]. But it is still deeply offensive to same-sex partners to have our relationships compared to bestiality. It is also absurd. Marriage is a legal contract between consenting adults and there is no proposal to give pets or household items legal standing to sign contracts. Needless to say, there are no examples of marriage equality leading to human/animal marriages overseas.

The argument that same-sex marriages will lead to polygamy (one man and several women) or polyamory (several people each in a relationship with all the others) is presented and taken a little more seriously. For example, conservative commentator, Andrew Bolt, believes that if personal freedom, equality and anti-discrimination are the principles behind same-sex marriage there is nothing to stop these principles being extended to multiple-partner relationships:

"When you destroy the traditional idea of a marriage being between a man and a woman, in favour of a union between any two consenting adults, you invite more changes. Why stop at two? Why not also "respect" unions between a man and two women?....If your choice of partner is entirely a private matter, and state intrusion on that silly and petty...why not allow polygamy? Isn't that the true libertarian position?" [114]

Marriage equality supporters often respond to such arguments by pointing out the holes in them. Take Michael Barnett whose marriage to his husband, Gregory Storer, featured in an episode of SBS's "Living with the enemy":

"All the polygamous marriages I've ever heard of are heterosexual – one man lots of wives. Where polygamy exists it is actually heterosexual marriage that has led to it. But no-one seriously suggests banning heterosexual marriage to prevent polygamy."

This is true, but the currency of the polygamy argument demands a more detailed response. While it's undeniable that marriage equality is about core principles like equality and freedom, it is not only about them. There are also pre-existing legal and cultural conditions which put firm constraints on how far reform can and should go.

Indeed, they put same-sex marriage and multiple-partner marriages at either end of the marriage spectrum.

Let's begin with polygamy. In none of the countries that allow same-sex marriage are polygamous marriages officially solemnised, even though some of them, like Spain, the Netherlands and the US, have large religious minorities that traditionally allow it[115]. There is an even wider gulf between the two issues in countries that allow polygamy. In places like Saudi Arabia, Afghanistan and Nigeria, homosexuals are not only unable to marry, they are put to death*.

This is not a coincidence. Polygamy is generally about one man controlling the lives of several women. It is an arrangement that comes from a time when women were considered less valuable than men, restricted to the house and to childrearing, and made their husband's property. This is reflected in the legal status of the wives in most polygamous relationships. Generally they lose their rights and autonomy when they marry, are punished much more harshly for adultery, and face more obstacles than men when seeking a divorce.

Wherever values like this prevail same-sex marriage is inconceivable. Where all husbands are legally dominant and all wives mere submissive extensions of their husband, it is absurd and profoundly threatening for there to be an

---

* One of the ironies of the Australian marriage equality debate is that polygamous marriages from such countries have been recognised for decades in Australian law to protect the legal rights of women in these marriages, whereas overseas same-sex marriages are not recognised at all. Needless to say, this recognition has never led to polygamous marriages being performed in Australia.

official union between two husbands or two wives. Where marriage is the union of a bread winner who must always be male and a child-carer who must always be female, it is economically unsustainable for households to be headed by two people of the same sex.

Same-sex marriage only begins to make sense in a society where there is a degree of social and economic equity between men and women, and legal equality between marriage partners. It only becomes possible for two men or two women to marry if men and women are already free to choose how they lead their lives regardless of their gender. In such a situation, polygamy as traditionally practised, is virtually inconceivable.

The situation is similar for polyamory. No polyamorous relationship has been recognised as a marriage anywhere same-sex marriages are permitted. A handful of polyamorous partners have raised the issue of legal or social recognition, but even they have shied away from marriage because it is too "conventional". Opponents of marriage equality will say it's too early to rule out the possibility of polyamorous marriages. But I confidently can, for two reasons.

The first is legal. All laws to do with personal relationships, from workplace entitlements through pensions to property division and child custody, are based on these relationships being a two-person deal. Hundreds of federal and state laws would need to be fundamentally altered to accommodate polyamorous marriages. That's assuming it is even possible to determine the existence and duration of a relationship, and the rights and responsibilities of the people in that relationship, where there are multiple partners who have come to, and departed from, the union at different times, and made differing contributions. It is particularly difficult to see how disputes about property division, or child custody and maintenance, could be resolved in the event of the relationship's breakdown, in part or whole. Not surprisingly, there is no body of law anywhere in the world that provides a precedent for this.

The second reason is cultural. Multiple partner relationships do not correspond to the understanding most people in western nations, including Australia, have of marriage. Same-sex marriages clearly do. This is why there is strong public support for same-sex marriage in all western countries including Australia but no discernable support for the recognition of polyamorous relationships as marriages.

In making his slippery slope argument against marriage equality, Andrew Bolt does something he frequently denounces the left for: he extrapolates a small set of examples and a much larger set of assumptions to their logical conclusion without bothering to refer back to the messy, complex facts of human law, culture and history. In doing so he manufactures a theoretical dystopia as abstract and nonsensical as the left wing utopias he makes fun of. The other opponents of marriage equality I have cited do the same. And, like many people swept up in ideology, they end up blind to their own original principles: the ACL to the religious freedom marriage equality will provide many faith communities, O'Neill to the freedom it gives the individual and Bolt to the traditional values it fosters. In this respect Andrew Bolt's sister, Stephanie, is a far better conservative than he is because she understands that valuable traditional institutions like marriage are "organic", not constrained by arid logic, and need to adapt if they are to thrive. She has written,

"Marriage is touted as one of our most enduring traditions. Traditions are organic; their foundations are laid in the past but they grow and evolve over time. Granting me and my partner the right to marry—to have our loving and committed relationship recognised in law and by the community—doesn't erode that tradition; it builds upon it." [116]

The Australian people, too, know ungrounded fear when they see it. When the Liberal Party's go-to research company, Crosby/Textor, asked about the "unintended consequences" of marriage equality that I've cited in this chapter and others, they found little concern among the ordinary Australians they surveyed. According to their research,

- less than 30% of Australians believe children need both a father and mother and legalising same-sex marriage could break this down

- less than 25% believe same-sex marriage undermines an institution that is already under threat

- only 22% believe same-sex marriages could devalue traditional marriages

- only 16% believe same-sex marriage will threaten religious freedoms, and

- only 17% believe allowing same-sex marriages is a slippery slope to polygamy

Predictions that marriage equality will have any number of fearful "unintended consequences" aren't borne out by a calm assessment of the facts. Examples cited to justify these predictions are tiny in number and mostly irrelevant. The circumstances that mitigate against bad outcomes are too-often ignored. Most Australians grasp this even if those commentators and advocates infatuated by their own logic don't. History shows that exaggeration about the negative impact of key reforms is common. From the emancipation of religious minorities in Europe in the Nineteenth Century, through votes for women and racial desegregation in the American south, there have been apocalyptic predictions about the privileged losing their freedoms, and society descending into authoritarianism or chaos. Yet most of us look with unmitigated pride on these milestones in the advancement of society. Our descendants will look back on marriage equality in the same way. And, like us, they will wonder at those fears which always seem to accompany change and which always come to nothing.

8. The alternatives don't offer full equality or recognition

"As I listened to the arguments that said that the state could legally recognise same-sex relationships but not call it 'marriage', I became less and less comfortable with that position. In the end it began to sound snobby. It began to sound as though the underlying message was 'Please don't let them into our exclusive club'. 'Please reserve this badge of honour for our group only, and exclude them'."

Rev Nathan Nettleton [117]

As we saw in chapter 2, existing laws that deem cohabiting same-sex couples to be de facto partners do not provide these partners with the legal security that comes with a marriage certificate. To address this problem, while maintaining the ban on same-sex marriage, some people advocate other ways to legally recognise same-sex unions. Here I'm talking about the kind of people who ask "why do you need to use the word 'marriage'?", in much the same exasperated way black or disabled people were once asked why they insisted on using the front door.

Some of the sillier proposals for avoiding use of the "m" word, include "garriage" (a contraction of "gay marriage"), "sarriage" (a contraction of "same-sex marriage"), "egairram" ("marriage" backwards), "nuptualisation" (a candidate for the ugliest noun-to-verb conversion ever) and "homosexual contract". Fortunately, none of these have advanced further than letters to the editor. The term that has entered legal lexicon as a substitute for marriage is "civil union" (I use the term "civil union" as a generic term that includes a registered partnership, a civil partnership, a Deed of Relationship and all other formally-recognised personal unions that are not marriages). Regardless of the term used, creating a substitute for equality in marriage creates an entirely new set of problems. As the international experience has shown, civil unions fail to provide the rights they are meant to guarantee and further entrench the discrimination they are meant to remove.

Like de facto partnerships, civil unions do not offer the same legal benefits as marriage, even when the law says they should. This is because they are not as widely understood or respected. Several inquiries into the operation of civil union schemes in Europe and North America confirm the conclusion of the 2008 New Jersey Civil Union Review Commission[118]:

"A common theme in the testimony gathered by the Commission was that while marriage is universally recognized by the public, civil union status must be explained repeatedly to employers, doctors, nurses, insurers, teachers, soccer coaches, emergency room personnel and the children of civil union partners. The testimony suggests that the need to explain the legal significance of civil union status to decision makers and individuals who provide vital services is more than a mere inconvenience....comments (were) provided by many witnesses regarding medical personnel, school officials and government workers who denied access and decision-making authority to civil union partners, either initially or completely, because of a lack of understanding of the rights that flow from civil unions." [119]

A low level of recognition is also a problem when it comes to "portability". In some cases, local or state civil unions aren't recognised in other states or nationally. National civil union schemes rarely provide rights in other countries.

But even if a solution can be found to these practical problems, legal unions other than marriage do not give same-sex couples the respect and acknowledgment that comes with marriage.

Kim Burman explains how a status other than marriage fails to do justice to the reality of deep marriage-like love, commitment and mutual responsibility between some same-sex partners.

"I live with the person I love, who is also female. According to the new laws, she is my 'partner'. But I really don't think that that term even begins to describe what we have together. Our relationship has survived everything that has tried to pull us apart. We survived when I moved to a new state, with no money or work....In turn, I support her now, when she cannot work due to an injury. I take care of her on the days that she is in too much pain to move. I drive her to all her appointments, and I console her on the days when it's all too much. I love her, and I would be honoured to call her My Wife. Is this extraordinary? No. It's just what any couple should do for each other. We have our good times, and our bad times, and we stick together always. How are we less than worthy? How are we not enough?"

As well as not necessarily connoting depth of attachment, civil unions do not necessarily carry the expectation partners will share their lives completely or the hope of a lifelong union. Neither do they signify inclusion within families or create kinship between them. There is not even an accepted civil union equivalent of the verb "to marry". In the words of American marriage equality advocate, Beth Robinson, "nobody writes songs about civil unions"[120].

Worse still, civil unions may actually downgrade the status of same-sex relationships.

The Massachusetts Supreme Court, like many courts across North America, has confirmed that the right of equal treatment is not only left unsatisfied by civil union schemes, but is breached by them.

"The dissimilitude between the terms 'civil marriage' and 'civil union' is not innocuous; it is a considered choice of language that reflects a demonstrable assigning of same-sex couples to second class status." [121]

Civil rights historians like Barbara Cox have drawn the parallel between civil unions and those former "Jim Crow laws" in the American south which enforced racial segregation.

"...restricting same-sex couples to civil unions is reminiscent of the racism that relegated African-Americans to separate railroad cars and separate schools. Our society's experiences with "separate and equal" have shown that separation can never result in equality because the separation is based on a belief that a distance needs to be maintained between those in the privileged position and those placed in the inferior position." [122]

Witnesses at the New Jersey civil union inquiry mentioned above see the effects of this second-class status on a daily basis.

"Witnesses called the two-tier system created by the Civil Union Act 'an invitation to discriminate' and a 'justification

to employers and others' to treat same-sex couples as 'less than' married couples... According to the testimony, the Civil Union Act amounts to a tacit endorsement of discriminatory treatment."

"Many witnesses noted that the labeling of civil union couples, not as married but in a civil union, has a detrimental effect on their families, showing children that their parents are different or somehow less than others, which can lead to teasing and bullying. Many witnesses observed that when the government treats people differently, it emboldens private citizens of any age to follow suit." [123]

For Stephanie Bolt, sister of conservative commentator and marriage equality opponent, Andrew Bolt, the issue is simple. She understands the appeal of civil unions to those seeking a resolution of the marriage equality debate. But this makes them no less damaging.

"Offering civil unions seems a reasonable compromise from the position of any straight person who has not ever had to question for a single moment others' acceptance of their relationship or their right to choose to marry the person they love. Offering civil unions sends a signal that, to me, says I am lesser." [124]

Civil unions have not only left unfulfilled their promise of equal rights and respect for same-sex couples, they appear to have made matters worse. Instead of eliminating discrimination they have entrenched it. Instead of removing stigma they have inflamed it. Instead of being a step towards full equality they are a step away.

This is probably why same-sex couples consistently show they prefer marriage to other forms of legal recognition.

Professor Lee Badgett conducted a study in 2008 which compared take-up rates for civil unions and marriage across those US states where one or the other was available to same-sex couples. The result was a higher take-up rate for marriage[125].

This is consistent with the results of the *Not So Private Lives* survey[126]. It showed that 55.4% of respondents who were in a same-sex de facto relationship would marry under Australian law if they had the choice. 25.6% would choose to be in a civil union, and only 17.7% would remain as de facto partners. Of those respondents currently in a state same-sex civil union, 78.3% would prefer to be married under Australian law. 60% of those in an overseas civil union or overseas same-sex marriage would prefer to be married in Australia.

Alternatives to marriage are important for providing legal security and/or formal recognition for those partners who do not wish to marry. In Australia we are lucky to have much stronger legal protections for cohabiting de facto couples than exist in countries such as Britain and the United States. We also have state civil union schemes which are some of the best in the world. They provide access to almost all spousal rights at both a local and national level. They provide these rights to a wider range of personal relationships, and with greater ceremonial recognition, than virtually all civil union schemes internationally (for more see chapter 15). But there is one piece missing from the jigsaw of legal options available to Australian couples. That piece is marriage for same-sex partners. The picture is not complete until that piece is in place, and that place can be taken by no other piece.

9. Marriage equality is urgent

"Tori and his partner of 14 years, Thomas, could never be married, not in Australia. Tori and Thomas deserved the same rights as other Australians. But that right was denied them, and now, for Tori, it's too late."

James Peron on Sydney siege hero, Tori Johnson[127]

The last objection to marriage equality, when every other has failed, is that it isn't urgent. Campaigners against the reform label it a distraction from more important issues such as jobs, health care, and the cost of living, a low priority for voters and a waste of parliament's time. This excuse often echoes from the mouths of politicians seeking to avoid any controversy. Of course, that's not the only excuse politicians use. They also commonly declare "we need to wait until there is a community consensus", "Australia won't be ready for this for a few years", "my leader doesn't support it", "my electorate doesn't support it", and even "same-sex marriage in other countries is the solution because Australian same-sex couples can all marry over there". Rarely have politicians seeking to abdicate responsibility found so many ways to say "not me, not here, not now".

But the alleged low priority of marriage equality is the point most often heard so let's address that. It's true most voters list jobs and health as higher priorities[128]. This is what you would expect given how fundamental such things are to so many people. I imagine same-sex partners would give them a high priority too. But the choice is a false one. The public has debated marriage equality for a decade without losing sight of other issues. Bills for marriage equality are typically just a few lines. Parliament has spent a tiny fraction of its time debating them. There has been no "distraction".[124]

It's hard to keep a straight face when opponents of marriage equality cry "low priority" and "waste of time", given their preoccupation with the issue. A study of Australian Christian Lobby media releases from 2012 found it is fixated on marriage equality and other LGBTI issues, mentioning them five times more often than the next most-mentioned issue, human trafficking, and more often than poverty, war, education, the economy and the Bible combined[129]. If it wasn't for the obsessive resistance of groups like the ACL, marriage equality would have been off the public and parliamentary agenda years ago. The best way to make the issue go away now is for parliament to listen to the people and pass it. It could be enacted in a few hours and would be forgotten within the month by all except those it directly affects.

But pulling apart the "waste-of-time" case against marriage equality isn't enough. Every argument against marriage equality appeals by design or default to some deep and often unacknowledged fear or prejudice: concern about children being raised by same-sex couples taps into a declining, but persistent, association between homosexuality and child abuse; concern about the slippery slope from marriage equality to polygamy or bestiality relies on the assumption same-sex relationships are perverse enough to lead directly to other perversions. In the same way, declaring marriage equality a distraction appeals to the fear that talking about homosexuality somehow promotes it. This fear once cast a pall of silence over homosexuality and made LGBTI people invisible. Today, it underlies laws against promoting and encouraging homosexuality in countries like Russia. To overcome the influence of such deep-set fears you need more than logic. As I've tried to show throughout this book, you need real stories from real people. Here is one such story:

"In 2012 I spoke to the Tasmanian Parliament about my family, and how I was lucky enough to be raised by two loving mums. I shared with politicians that one of my mothers was terminally ill. I asked them to allow my mums to be united, before death parted them forever. Sadly the majority didn't open their hearts to the importance of marriage to my family. Now the deep love and commitment shared by my mothers will never be recognised for what it really was - a devoted marriage. This is a regret I will always carry, not least on the day I marry the woman I love. It simply makes no sense to me that the two people who taught me what commitment means could never marry like I can. As a teacher, I also worry about what message it sends our children when the law says some people have fewer rights just because of who they love. I hear people say marriage equality can wait, but not for families like mine."

Nick Outterside, a teacher from North West Tasmania, wrote these words in 2013, not long after the death of one of the women who had raised him. Nick speaks on behalf of the many Australians for whom marriage equality will come too late: for the children who will never see their parent's relationships treated with equal respect, the parents who will never be able to walk their child down the aisle, and for the partners whose chance of marriage to the one they loved most in the world is gone forever.

For people facing these possibilities right now, marriage equality is desperately urgent. In March 2014, a few days after his partner almost died following cancer surgery, Greg Lovett wrote to his local MP about marriage equality. Greg took particular issue with the MP's go-slow on the issue.

*"This terrible time has provided constant reminders of the lesser rights we hold in Australia...with each new contact requiring me to explain my partnership and next of kin role. If we held equal rights our relationship could not be questioned. My role as next of kin would not need re-stating. Your view of Same Sex Marriage has been quoted as, "I think it's an idea whose time hasn't quite come". It's time Australia was fair to us and gave us equal rights, not in the future, but **now**."*

Following the recovery of Greg's partner, and as soon as UK marriages became possible in Australia, the couple took advantage of Greg's dual citizenship and married in the UK High Commission in Canberra.

It's not just injury or disease that make marriage equality urgent for some Australians. It's urgent for people vulnerable to the stigma and discrimination perpetuated by exclusion from marriage, like the young man whose suicide attempt I recounted in chapter 3. It's urgent for those partners who miss out on legal entitlements and protections, like the soldier whose story is found in chapter 2.

Most of all, it's urgent for Australia as a whole. Every time another country adopts marriage equality Australia's reputation for tolerance suffers a little more and we are seen as a little more backward and benighted. If our leaders' indifference to marriage equality continues, Australia's failure to enact marriage equality will come to define us and set us apart from other western countries. That point may well be closer than we think. Following the successful marriage equality referendum in the Republic of Ireland in May 2015, Australia is the only developed English-speaking country without the reform. The cumulative damage to our national image from delaying marriage equality will take a long time to undo. I can confidently predict this because I saw first-hand how deeply Tasmania's reputation suffered from being the last Australian state to decriminalise homosexuality. Tasmania's damaged reputation took almost a generation to repair. Australia's could too.

What makes this situation even more bewildering is that three quarters of Australians believe marriage equality is inevitable. This is higher than the percentage of Australians who support the reform so it must include people who concede history's verdict will be different to their own. If, as the vast number of Australians agree, marriage equality will happen, why delay it any longer? If exclusion from marriage is doomed why perpetuate the pain it causes? If same-sex marriages are bound to happen in Australia why deny these marriages only to those couples for whom it may soon be too late.

10. There is strong and growing support for equality

"Society evolves. Social attitudes change...To future generations the prohibition on same-sex marriage will seem as unfathomable as the prohibition on interracial marriage seems today. The stark question for each of us is, which side of history do we want to be on?"

Australian marriage equality advocate, Tony Pitman[130]

We have seen how marriage equality is a matter of basic human rights, how same-sex couples and their families benefit legally and socially from this equality, and how marriage itself is uplifted not diminished by embracing loving, committed couples regardless of gender.

We have seen that same-sex relationships are equal in their capacity for love and commitment, that marriage has changed over the years so that the recognition of such love and commitment is now its primary purpose, and that while marriage still has associations with religion and the raising of children these are arguments for equality, not against it.

For all these reasons and many more, support for marriage equality is steadily growing. Twenty-one nations, including South Africa, Spain, Portugal and Argentina, and thirty-seven US states, including Alabama, Oklahoma and Utah, allowed same-sex marriage *at the time of writing*[131]. This caveat is important because the number is also accelerating. Among comparable countries, Australia is alone. Same-sex couples can marry in Canada, New Zealand, the UK, Ireland and the US.

In an increasing number of these countries marriage equality has been achieved by conservative governments. This includes New Zealand and the UK. The conservative case for marriage equality was given perhaps its strongest exposition by the Conservative Prime Minister of Great Britain, David Cameron, when he said,

"Conservatives believe in the ties that bind us; that society is stronger when we make vows to each other and support each other. So I don't support gay marriage despite being a Conservative. I support gay marriage because I'm a Conservative." [132]

The growing cross-party support for marriage equality overseas highlights the lack of political leadership on the issue in Australia and feeds a growing perception in other western countries that Australia is backward, at least politically. There is a corresponding embarrassment felt by many Australians about our growing isolation. In the words of Johnathon Parker:

"I have a great desire to one day be able to marry a partner of my choosing - and have that marriage fully and equally recognised by the law in this great country that I love. I consider Australia to be a forward thinking, modern country of pioneers and innovators, however, on this particular issue, Australia seems to be being left behind."

But despite Australian politicians lagging behind their counterparts elsewhere, support beyond Capital Hill is strong.

The number of corporations, local government authorities, unions, and community groups that support marriage equality is rapidly increasing[133]. Even Government agencies are beginning to acknowledge the reality of same-sex marriages; in 2011 the Australian Bureau of Statistics counted same-sex married couples in the national Census for the first time[134].

In turn, this shift in organisational support reflects a shift in public opinion. In 2004 a Newspoll found that 38% of Australians supported marriage equality while 44% opposed[135]. In 2007 a Galaxy Poll found 57% of those surveyed support marriage equality[136]. A Galaxy Poll conducted in 2009 using an identical question to 2007, showed 60% of those surveyed were in favour of marriage equality, with a clear majority of support among voters for both of Australia's major parties[137]. By 2012 this had increased to 65%. The most recent figure, from a national survey by prominent research company, Crosby Textor, found 72% support. Not even in some countries with marriage equality is support this high. Just as importantly, there was more support for marriage equality than opposition to it in every demographic, including the elderly, people in rural and regional areas and Christians.

Support is particularly high among young voters. This may be because they are more familiar with, and accepting of, LGBTI people. It may also be because they are part of what I call the Family Law Act Generation – people born after reform to marriage, divorce and de facto laws gave the sexes greater legal equity and made marriage a couple's choice rather than society's requirement. The possibility of same-sex marriages arises directly from both these developments. (for more on this see chapter 11). But young people are not alone. Married Australians raising children also support marriage equality in high numbers, perhaps because they have such an immediate experience of the value of marriage for children and family life. Whatever the reasons, on the trends indicated by these polls, we can expect support for marriage equality to keep on increasing.

In the LGBTI community, support is also high. The *Not So Private Lives* study[138], found 80% of same-sex partners support their right to marry and a majority - 55.4% - would marry if they had the choice, a figure that increases to over 80% among same-sex couples with young children[139]. Support is also significantly higher, again, among the young. This may be because older LGBTI people grew up when legally-recognised same-sex marriage was inconceivable. It may be because, in the past, gay identity was defined in a way which made a virtue out of our exclusion from marriage (for more on this see chapter 15). Or it may simply be because young LGBTI people are also part of a generation for whom marriage no longer looms large as life's only legitimate path.

Clearly, those who declare the Australian people do not support marriage equality, or that the LGBTI community is divided on the issue, are wrong. So, why then do a majority of Australian politicians still oppose marriage equality?

In Australia the answer is this: politicians believe those who oppose reform are more committed and passionate than those who support, including, crucially, at the ballot box. This perception is beginning to change. A 2004 Senate inquiry into marriage equality received 13,000 submissions of which less than a quarter supported reform. A 2009 inquiry received 27,000 with 11,000 in favour of equality[140]. By 2012 the scales had tipped. In that year two inquiries received over a quarter of a million submissions, 64% of which argued for marriage equality. This change corresponded to a dramatic but little-noticed shift in opinion polls. Between 2009 and 2012 a significant proportion of Australians moved from simply being supporters of marriage equality to being strong supporters. Clearly, supporters of reform have become more passionate, but still the minority who oppose change remain the most vocal.

In Australia there is no charter of human rights to allow courts to consider marriage equality as courts overseas have. There are no citizen-initiated referenda to allow the majority of fair-minded and tolerant Australians to directly change the law (for more, see chapter 12). Marriage equality will only be achieved when those Australians who support reform make their views known to their family members, friends, workmates and, most important of all, to their elected representatives through letters, through personal conversations and through their ballots (see chapter 13). Marriage equality will only occur when each of us chooses which side of history we will be on, and acts on that choice. In the next section of this book I look at how each of us can best put our support for marriage equality into action.

REFLECTIONS ON THE

AUSTRALIAN MARRIAGE

EQUALITY DEBATE

Introduction to section two

The Australian marriage equality debate is over a decade old. It predates equivalent community debates in some other countries, including the UK and New Zealand, that have already achieved marriage equality.

The protracted nature of the debate naturally prompts people on both sides to ask whence the debate arose, what propels it and how can it be resolved. I know from my own experience as a marriage equality advocate that these questions occupy the minds of ordinary Australians at least as much as the question addressed in the previous section of this book, should same-sex couples be able to marry?

In this section I set out to address some of these common questions about the marriage equality debate. In the first chapter I look at the deep cultural and demographic trends that have generated it. In the second, I consider the merits of the different paths towards allowing same-sex couples to marry. In the third chapter I look at what individuals and groups can do to move marriage equality forward.

11. Why is Australia debating marriage equality?

Australia's political debate on marriage equality, and the community campaign to secure it, go back to 2004 when the Howard Government amended the Marriage Act to explicitly state that marriage is only between a man and a woman and ban the recognition of overseas same-sex marriages. Until then the restriction of wedlock to heterosexual couples was inferred from centuries of court decisions.

What challenged these judicial precedents was the enactment of marriage equality in several Canadian provinces in 2003. Among the Australian couples married in Canada that year were two who asked the Federal Court of Australia to recognise their recently-made vows. Opponents of marriage equality feared the couples might succeed, given Australia's liberal foreign marriage recognition laws. Pragmatists in the Liberal Government saw an opportunity to corral evangelical voters in key marginal seats and wedge Labor, in much the same way George Bush's Republicans were then uniting conservatives and dividing the Democrats by pushing constitutional bans on same-sex marriage. Labor avoided the wedge by uniting behind the proposed ban. The Greens took up marriage equality as a flagship issue. Amidst impassioned speeches for and against, a ban on same-sex marriage passed the parliament in August 2004 (for more on the events of 2004 see chapter 14).

The partisan power plays that accompanied the birth of the contemporary marriage equality debate have led sceptics of the reform, on the right and left, to denigrate it as a confected distraction from more important issues.

Groups like the Australian Christian Lobby believe marriage equality is only an issue because the Greens keep pushing it. Left wing commentators like Guy Rundle have dismissed it as a trick to keep suburban battlers voting Liberal (see chapter 15 for more). Publicists on both sides of politics have repeatedly dismissed marriage equality as an elite concern, despite record numbers of submissions to parliament on the issue, or "not part of the narrative" despite the constant national conversation. For them all, marriage equality is blown backwards and forward by politicians' hot air, not the surer winds of social change.

In reality, the marriage-like features of same-sex relationships and the aspiration of same-sex couples to marry have a long history. So do the legal, social and cultural changes that made marriage equality not just plausible but inevitable[141].

"Keep faith"

Colonial officials obsessing over homosexuality among Australia's convicts wrote of male and female same-sex couples behaving as husband and wife. The one male-to-male convict love letter we have does not deal in these traditional marital gender roles, but it does express a selfless and exclusive marriage-like commitment between the partners. Facing imminent execution the anonymous convict declares,

"Dear Jack I value Death nothing but it is in leaving you my dear behind and no one to look after you.... The only thing that grieves me love is when I think of the pleasant nights we have had together. I hope you wont fall in love with no other man when I am dead and I remain your True and loving affectionate Lover".

The same devoted, conjugal commitment is to be found in the biographies of many other same-sex attracted Australians. The final wish of bushranger Andrew Scott, aka, Captain Moonlight was to be buried with the man with whom he was "one in hopes, in heart and soul and this unity lasted until he died in my arms". Novelist, feminist and Christian Marie Bjelke-Petersen declared of her life-long partner, Sylvia Mills, "God's Angels often come in human form not as strangers whose lips never touch ours…but as friends, close dear friends, whom we may fondle & caress & feel they really belong to us".

From the first half of the Twentieth Century there are written and photographic records of same-sex couples marrying in unofficial commitment ceremonies. A lesbian couple, Paddy and Robbie Byrnes, married themselves in 1956 in a private ceremony in a church. Paddy wrote,

"On 17 March 1956 we became as one in a wee church, after lighting two candles and exchanging wedding rings inscribed 'Keep Faith'" [142].

The record swells with the advent of gay newspapers. A news item in a 1973 edition of the Camp Inc newsletter notes,

"Two homosexual girls in Brisbane have married, and two men in Sydney wanted to marry a few months ago. Camp Inc searched around for a minister, many said they would but were afraid…Finally a 75-year-old Presbyterian minister said he'd marry the men."

Gay liberation in the early 1970s opened up more opportunities for same-sex couples seeking to marry. As the Camp Inc story shows this included religious ceremonies in gay and gay-friendly churches. It also included the push for official recognition. In 1975 Australian, Anthony Sullivan, and his American partner, Richard Adams, were among six couples married in Colorado after a local county clerk found there was nothing in state law to stop her issuing same-sex marriage licences. "It was a day and age in which anything was possible", Sullivan later recalled of those figures like Rosa Parks and Martin Luther King who had inspired him. The marriages were never voided but Sullivan's application for American residency was rejected on the ground that he had "failed to establish that a bona fide marital relationship can exist between two faggots"[143].

Some gay liberationists offered a critique of marriage as an out-dated, oppressive institution that same-sex relationships should be better than, not limited by. Inheritors of that idea see today's marriage equality movement as a betrayal of the gay movement's origins (for more see chapter 15). But gay lib was many things. It could be as easily said that their wholesale rejection of marriage was a quixotic detour from the civil rights path trod by people like Anthony Sullivan.

When gay men began to die from AIDS a decade after Sullivan's marriage the importance of legally-recognising same-sex relationships was highlighted by the failure of the law to treat same-sex partners as next-of-kin. In America this brought the demand for marriage equality into focus. But in Australia it seems to have had the opposite effect. Australia had a far better developed system for recognising unmarried, de facto relationships than the US. With urgency and achievability to justify them, Australian activists and law-makers focused exclusively on expanding de facto laws to include same-sex relationships. Pioneering groups like Homodefactos grew out of the failure of superannuation funds to recognise the partners of gay men dead from AIDS. The first law recognising same-sex relationships was the Tasmanian HIV/AIDS Preventative Measures Act 1993. Other factors at play were the failure of the Australian gay rights movement to develop the national voice necessary to lobby for a national reform, and its continued links to a Labor Party that saw de facto laws as its great achievement and marriage as a culture war minefield. The low expectations of a minority buffeted by bigotry for too long also figured. Still today, young same-sex couples are more likely than their elders to want to wed, partly because it was an aspiration older gays accustomed themselves not to expect, or defined their sexuality against. For all these reasons, marriage equality was consistently and deliberately sidelined as "just symbolic" and "a distraction" by those who would have been its advocates under different circumstances. I know because I was one of the advocates who played along, with great ambivalence, to secure some legal protections for same-sex partners. The deal paid its dividend with the relatively rapid recognition of same-sex financial and workplace entitlements. But the price was that the Australian marriage equality debate was years behind comparable countries like the US and Canada when it finally began, and the initiative was handed to those who opposed reform.

"A love match"

Up to this point we've seen that the perception same-sex relationships are marriage-like, and the aspiration to have this recognised, go back far beyond 2004, even if political ideology and expediency have sometimes submerged them. But the history of marriage equality is also about the history of marriage, and the intimate lives of the millions of heterosexuals who have contributed to its evolution despite "defenders of marriage" trying to hold change back.

As recently as forty years ago marriage was very different to what it is today. At the weddings I attended as a child it was considered scandalous for the marrying couple to have lived together or for the bride not to wear white, for the couple to write their own vows or marry in a garden, or for the bride not to take her husband's family name and plan to give up her job. Those who muttered disapproval at such innovations thought of marriage as a compulsory pre-requisite to sex and procreation, a relationship between two partners whose contribution to the union was based on strictly defined gender roles, and a ritual that had to take place in church and preferably between members of the same faith.

In marked contrast, today it is common for couples to have an established relationship before they wed. Most women feel the job they take and the name they have is their choice, along with how many children they have and when they have them. A church wedding is also a choice, with the result that it is remarkable for couples not to marry in gardens. Just as heterosexual couples decide why and when they marry and how to conduct their marriage, they also decide if and when to end it through divorce.

Many different factors have contributed to these changes: laws protecting de facto partners and allowing no fault divorce, accessible, effective contraception, legal equality and growing economic equality between men and women, and the decline in religious adherence. Together, the effect of these changes has been to make the idea of same-sex marriages not only conceivable but hard to avoid. With marriage now a choice for heterosexual couples, why are same-sex couples denied the same choice? If gender makes no critical difference to what partners bring to a marriage, why do marriages have to be between a man and a woman? If marriages matter just as much without a religious blessing, why deny marriage to those some religions curse? It is not LGBTI people who seek to change marriage. Married heterosexuals themselves have developed the idea of matrimony to the point where same-sex relationships fit comfortably within it. In the words of Sydney Morning Herald columnist, Adele Horan,

"Marriage is more than ever a love match between equals, a primarily personal relationship in which partners maintain a level of independence. They organise their partnership on the basis of personal inclination rather than gender roles, although no one says that battle is won; they value the right to decide whether to have children or not. Is it any wonder that gays and lesbians are saying 'Hey, that describes us'?" [144]

It always surprises me that some older feminists and progressives, who championed marriage reform in the past, are indifferent or disdainful to the idea of same-sex marriage when they should see it as their diadem (see chapter 15 for more). The same goes for those Christian conservatives who lament the "long decline" of marriage but react to same-sex marriage as if it is a uniquely serious threat that sprang from nowhere and can be driven back there.

Wallflowers no longer

The long-held aspiration of same-sex couples to marry, and the evolution of marriage to meet that aspiration, are necessary to explain the origins of the marriage equality debate, but they are not sufficient. In the final years of the Twentieth Century two more critical preconditions to the current marriage equality debate brought together broader social trends. They were a growing familiarity with same-sex relationships among the majority of Australians and a boom in gay parenting.

Tolerance of same-sex relationships compounds itself. As same-sex unions are destigmatised so it is easier for same-sex partners to come out, further reducing the stigma. Studies from the US have shown that when heterosexuals work with or are related to an LGBTI person they are more likely to support marriage equality. But in my experience what has mattered more than just knowing someone who is LGBT or I is being familiar with their life. Growing tolerance has meant LGBTI people have more of a choice about staying in or moving to suburban, regional and rural communities. This is why the gay ghettoes in our major cities have stopped growing and may even be emptying. The demographic shift of LGBTI people out of the inner city is occurring across the Western world. In Australia we can see it in successive censuses showing the biggest proportional increases in the numbers of same-sex couples in places like North Queensland, northern NSW, central Victoria, south-west WA and Tasmania. What this means is more day-to-day interaction between same-sex couples and the majority of Australians. An elderly suburban heterosexual couple is today much more likely than their parents to have their gay child and her partner living around the corner. This proximity and familiarity does more than a hundred sitcoms or advertising campaigns to demonstrate how little real difference there is between same-sex and different-sex relationships, and, in turn, how absurd it is to exclude same-sex couples from marriage.

Arising from, and fostering, the perception of little real difference is the upsurge in same-sex couples raising children. As heterosexual Australians become more familiar with same-sex couples it is more widely accepted that children can thrive in their care. Laws governing access to fertility treatment, surrogacy and adoption have been reformed accordingly. So have laws and policies recognising the families thus created. In turn, seeing two-mum and two-dad families experience the same joys and trials as others promotes further empathy. As many as half of Australia's female couples and a quarter of our male couples are currently caring for children. The gay child of our elderly suburban couple is now many times more likely to be raising their grandchild than she would have been a generation ago. The intergenerational bonds thus created cannot long withstand lingering ignorance or prejudice.

It is not hard to see how an upsurge in gay parenting has fuelled the marriage equality debate. While there is no longer a strong legal link between marriage and children – two generations have passed since "bastard" children were legally penalised - there is still a strong cultural association. Marriage benefits children when it provides them with a sense of continuity, stability and normality. This is why the decision to have children is what prompts many heterosexual de facto couples to marry. The benefits of marriage for children flow equally to the children of same-sex couples. Arguably, they flow more, given the lingering stigma children of same-sex couples experience. This may be why polls show support for marriage equality among heterosexual couples with young children is well above the national average.

The upsurge in gay parenting has also seen the advent of a new set of very determined marriage equality advocates. Like other parents, gay parents want the best for their children. This includes the opportunity to live without prejudice, and the validation that can come with having married parents. As the children of same-sex couples grow into adulthood, they too, often become advocates for marriage equality. Many advocate eloquently for the right of their parents to marry, but it is the sheer fact of the normality that speaks loudest.

The late Christopher Pearson – a conservative Catholic columnist and celibate gay man - objected to marriage equality because LGBTI people "are wallflowers at the great dance of the generations". Thanks to the demographic shifts I've mentioned, this is increasingly out of line with the experience of heterosexual Australians. An excellent example is the world champion axeman and Tasmanian blue-collar icon, David Foster. Foster came out publicly for marriage equality in 2011, having previously opposed it quite strongly. In his own words what made the difference was his daughter coming out and bringing her partner and their daughter back to the Foster's hometown. Like millions of other Australians, Foster could see first-hand that his daughter's relationship exhibited the same qualities as his own marriage. His conclusion:

"She is a nurse, she has a beautiful partner and a child and if they wish to get married, I can't see why they can't. Marriage is about being in love and about family. They are in love and they are a family just like any other. I've been lucky enough to walk down the aisle with my eldest daughter, and I'd like to do the same with Sally." [145]

For David Foster, as for millions of other Australians, it has been a small step from understanding that same and different-sex relationships are equally loving and committed, to wanting them included in "the great dance" of which marriage is so integral a part.

12. What are the paths to allowing same-sex couples to legally marry in Australia?

Australian heterosexual couples marry under the federal Marriage Act. The obvious path to marriage equality runs directly through federal parliament and ends with the amendment of that Act to allow same-sex couples to marry. But currently that path is blocked. The Labor Party allows its members a conscience vote while the Liberal and National parties do not. This means no matter which party is in government there is an automatic majority against reform. In the words of commentator, George Megalogenis, parliament is "rigged" against marriage equality[146].

This is an anomalous situation. Labor, the party of collective action, is usually far less likely to have a conscience vote than the Coalition parties, which say they value personal freedom. Labor usually allows conscience votes only on life and death issues like abortion and euthanasia. In contrast, the Coalition parties have had conscience votes on a wide range of issues from compulsory voting and royal commissions to the site of the new parliament house, as well as fertility treatment, human cloning, abortion and euthanasia. Prior to the marriage equality debate, amendments to the Marriage and Family Law Acts were decided on conscience votes. Homosexual law reform has also been a matter of conscience for the Coalition parties. Between 1949 and 2007 there were thirty-two conscience votes in federal parliament, two thirds under Coalition governments. In the words of former NSW Liberal Senator, Chris Puplick,

"The Liberal Party has a long, honourable history of allowing its parliamentarians a 'conscience' vote on issues of moral/ ethical concern where there are divisions of opinion - genuinely held on all sides. The Liberal Party I joined in May 1965 prided itself on the right of its parliamentarians to vote according to their consciences. I hope with the passage of nearly 50 years that is still one of its core values." [147]

When it comes to marriage equality, Labor and the Coalition have reversed their traditional approach to conscience votes largely because of the strong religious caucuses within both federal parties. The Catholic caucus within Labor could not hold the Party back from adopting a pro-marriage equality policy in 2012. But it did extract a conscience vote as a concession. There is currently a push from grassroots Labor members to ensure all Labor MPs have to uphold party policy on marriage equality. It seems a fair objective given Labor candidates know the party they signed up to enforces strict discipline. But threats to split the Party over marriage equality, like the Party was split over Communism in the 1950s, could be enough to dampen the campaign. A Coalition conscience vote is more likely, but is still stiffly resisted by its religious caucus, some members of which have also resorted to intimidating and misinforming backbenchers. For example, they have put around that the Liberal and National parties only allow conscience votes on matters of life and death. This is wrong. As I've noted, the Coalition has allowed a conscience vote on a wide range of issues. Fortunately, these Coalition marriage equality opponents defying their own Party's core values are not in the majority. They face not only supporters of the reform but opponents who support a conscience vote because it would be consistent with party principles and tradition. It will be these principled men and women who unrig parliament.

With a cross-party conscience vote marriage equality becomes possible, but still not inevitable. The powerful religious caucuses I've mentioned will do all they can to ensure a vote in parliament is delayed because, they say, the issue is a waste of parliament's time and there are more important problems to deal with like unemployment, education, the cost of living, "the economy" or anything else that is too intractable or amorphous to actually solve (see chapter 9 for more). Alternatively, they will bring the matter to a vote before their colleagues have had a chance to look carefully at the issues involved because, they say, the debate causes division in the community, the very division their own rhetoric has created. And, of course, when a vote finally comes, they will do all they can to induce or threaten their colleagues into voting "no", so that the vote risks becoming one of conscience in name only. In this situation it is prudent to consider other paths towards allowing same-sex couples to legally marry.

State same-sex marriage laws

In a federation like Australia the obvious alternative to reform at a federal level is reform through the states. In the Australian Constitution the power to make laws for marriage is shared between the federal and state governments. This is why all heterosexual marriages were solemnised under state laws up until the federal Marriage Act was passed in 1960. The first state to step on to the path of allowing same-sex couples to marry was Tasmania with a Greens' bill introduced by Nick McKim in 2005. Other states followed. Tasmania led again in 2012 with legislation that passed the Lower House but was narrowly defeated by two votes in the Upper House. The ACT then strode forward with a bill that passed its Assembly and became law. Australia's first same-sex marriages – 31 in total – were solemnised under that law until it was overturned by the High Court in December 2013.

In the minds of many, that was the end of the state route to same-sex marriages. But it wasn't, thanks to a critical difference between the Tasmanian and ACT bills. The ACT law drew on the definition of marriage from the federal Marriage Act. The ACT Government was warned by numerous legal experts that this was unconstitutional. It went ahead anyway. Reflecting the frustration of many advocates, former Australian Marriage Equality convener, Alex Greenwich, wrote to the ACT Government suggesting it was putting politics before people:

"Your legislation must be designed with one goal in mind; to protect the same-sex couples seeking to marry under it. It should not be considered as a piece of protest legislation against the Federal Government. I note that your government waited till the Coalition formed government to legislate in this regard, despite having the numbers and a mandate to pass legislation for over a year." [148]

In contrast, to the ACT statute, the Tasmanian bill established a distinct scheme for solemnising same-sex marriages that ran parallel to the federal Marriage Act but did not impinge on it at any point. This has been lauded as constitutionally sound by Australia's leading constitutional academic, Prof George Williams, and its leading constitutional barrister, Bret Walker SC. It is the model adopted by MPs in other states and territories, most recently Norfolk Island.

The experts agree that states *can* allow same-sex couples to marry. But there is also the broader question of whether they *should*. Sceptics have dismissed the idea of state laws allowing same-sex marriages because the marriage would only be recognised in the state that solemnised it, and because same-sex couples would marry under a statute specific to them, which makes it second-rate and not full equality. This latter point has even been extrapolated to the perverse conclusion that state same-sex marriage laws somehow discriminate against same-sex couples. This escape clause is characteristic of, but by no means limited to, conservative Catholic legislators who support social justice, just not for gays.

The first criticism fails to grasp why we have a federal system. It is designed to allow reform to move forward at one level if it fails at the other. In Australia, almost all reforms to laws governing relationships, including the recognition of de facto and same-sex relationships, have occurred first at a state level before being enacted federally. Why should same-sex marriage be any different? In all other federations where marriage equality has moved forward, including Canada, the US, Mexico, Argentina and Brasil, same-sex marriages occurred first at a state or provincial level. Why should Australia be any different? Yes, the first same-sex marriages would only be recognised in the state or territory of their solemnisation, but this didn't stop the first marriages in the ACT being as important to the partners concerned as marriages under a federal law. We can expect the first Australian state Same-Sex Marriage Act to be emulated quickly by governments in other states and federally. It is what has happened with other relationship law reforms. It is what couples from across Australia, married under the first state law, will loudly demand.

The second criticism – that marriage under a state law is unequal, second-rate and discriminatory - fails to grasp the aspiration at the core of the marriage equality movement; the choice to legally marry. Marrying partners do not particularly care which parliament enacted the statute under which they wed and how that statute is written. This was true of my parents who married under a state heterosexual marriage law in 1959 with markedly different provisions to such laws in other Australian states. It is true today for English same-sex couples who marry under a specific same-sex marriage law separate to the law under which their heterosexual counterparts wed. It was true of the couples who enthusiastically married in the ACT, and those who plan, just as keenly, to marry under other local laws not yet passed. In the words of Ivan Hinton-Teoh, who married under the ACT Marriage Equality ACT in 2013,

"the respect and affirmation I felt being able to legally marry Chris was no less because it was under a Territory law. In fact, it may have been greater because the law was created by a truly representative government, reflecting the acceptance and respect we enjoy from our community".[149]

Those who say they support the principle of marriage equality, but oppose state laws for being "unequal" or for "discriminating against same-sex couples", cut off their nose to spite their face. They echo those people who held back the emancipation of women and blacks out of a misplaced paternalistic concern for the welfare of these groups. Worst among them are those who oppose the principle of LGBTI equality until the moment it becomes a convenient excuse to vote against a state same-sex marriage law. The best I can say about them is they are like anti-Islamic bigots who are feminists for precisely as long as it takes to justify their opposition to burqas. Not surprisingly the pro-equality case against state same-sex marriages is most often heard from state legislators who want to have their electoral cake and eat it too by pleasing voters on both sides of the debate. But beneath their claim that a different statute means a second-rate marriage I detect homophobia as well as expediency. Only if you believe same-sex relationships are already less worthy would you label a marriage law specific to these couples less valuable than the heterosexual-specific law that currently prevails. The right to make solemn, legally-sanctioned vows of lifelong commitment and to have that commitment called marriage is what most same-sex couples want. A state law can meet that demand as well as a federal law.

Recognising overseas same-sex marriages

Another path to recognising at least some same-sex marriages in Australia is the recognition of overseas same-sex marriages. This was first proposed after marriage equality was achieved in New Zealand in 2013. Before that, most Australian same-sex couples who went overseas to marry did so in Canada, the US or Argentina where there are no residency requirements. A handful married in the Netherlands or Scandinavia where one partner must be a citizen. The Australian Government did its best to stop this happening. In 2004, at the same time as it entrenched marriage as a heterosexual union, it banned the recognition in Australian law of overseas same-sex marriages. The solemn, legal vows of lifelong commitment made by Australians in other countries were legally disregarded and disrespected when they returned to Australia, just because of the gender of the person to whom their vows were made. When this didn't stop couples marrying overseas, the Australian Government refused to issue its LGBTI citizens with the documents they needed to wed in other countries. Some overseas governments require a Certificate of Non-Impediment before they will allow a foreigner to marry. A CNI shows the person in question is of marrying age and not already married. Not allowing same-sex partners access to CNIs allowed the Australian Government to extend its prejudice across the globe. It also didn't work. Some foreign governments were so affronted by Canberra's interference with who married under their laws they waived the CNI requirement for Australians. Over 1300 same-sex couples indicated they had married overseas on the 2011 Census form, a significant under-estimate according to the Bureau of Statistics which also doesn't include expat Australians in same-sex marriages. In 2012, after Angela Borella, the sister of former Tasmanian Premier, David Bartlett, publicly revealed the Australian Government's rules stopped her from marrying her Portuguese partner, in Portugal under Portuguese law, the ban on CNIs was finally lifted (for more about the ban on CNIs see chapters 1 and 14).

But the ban on recognising overseas same-sex marriages in Australia remained. New Zealand is much closer to Australia than Portugal, geographically, culturally and economically. The expectation was that marriage equality in New Zealand would greatly increase the number of married same-sex partners – Australians who flew to NZ to marry, and New Zealanders resident in Australia – whose legal marriage would be ignored by the Australian authorities. This proved correct with almost 250 Australian couples marrying in the first year alone. There are no figures for the number of married LGBTI New Zealanders living in Australia. The legislation to remove the ban on recognising overseas same-sex marriages sought to provide these couples with the same dignity and respect as other married couples. It sought to stem the tide of Australian same-sex couples deciding to move to the country that gives them equality, as well as those same-sex couples from overseas who choose not to move to Australia because their marriage is not respected. It also sought to solve the practical legal problems faced by same-sex couples married overseas. A marriage certificate allows same-sex partners to prove their next-of-kin rights if challenged, but only if that marriage certificate has legal standing. On top of this, some countries only allow residents to divorce. This means same-sex partners married overseas but living in Australia can't divorce because neither the country they married in, nor the country they are living in, allows it (for more on this see chapter 2).

Some states have come to the rescue. Tasmania, Queensland and NSW recognise overseas same-sex marriages as state civil unions, which are in turn recognised as de facto relationships in federal law. This at least gives same-sex couples married overseas some legal protection. But it has also given rise to another problem. In 2014 the UK achieved marriage equality and the Australian Government consented to allowing same-sex couples to marry in UK consulates in Australia. This was a stark contrast to previous Australian governments that had banned foreign missions in Australia from conducting same-sex marriages. The Government's change of heart on consular marriages was welcomed because it allowed same-sex couples to marry at home with family and friends. However, as I note in chapter 2, the problem with UK marriages is that the UK recognises Australian civil unions as equivalent to UK civil partnerships and doesn't allow couples to be married and in a civil partnership. Suddenly, Australian same-sex partners in Australian state civil unions faced the choice of the respect and affirmation that comes with marriage and the practical legal benefits that come with a state civil union. No couple should have to make this choice. The problem would be solved by the Australian Government's recognition of overseas same-sex marriages for what they are – valid, legal marriages.

In 2014 a Senate inquiry rejected the recognition of overseas same-sex marriages out of hand. Dominated by Coalition and Labor Senators opposed to marriage equality, it condemned the move as a "backdoor" path to achieving marriage equality, despite the immediate benefits mentioned above. It also cited concerns that two tiers of same-sex relationships would be created, with same-sex couples who are poor, aged or on a pension disadvantaged because they cannot afford international travel. This echoes the sophists who say state same-sex marriage laws discriminate against and demean same-sex relationships. It ignores evidence that many same-sex partners are willing to make immense sacrifices to marry overseas because they value marriage so highly. It also ignores evidence that some of the couples most eager to marry, overseas if necessary, are those who are ailing and old and cannot wait for Australia's laws to change.

An excellent example is Lee and Sandra. Lee is terminally ill and the couple's final wish is to legally marry. Both worked as nurses but lost their savings when a builder they hired went broke. Both are on pensions and barely manage to pay for Lee's care. Sandra had to sell their campervan to pay for Lee's funeral arrangements. But still they made the sacrifices necessary to travel to New Zealand to marry. In Sandra's words it gave Lee something to look forward to and live for - "it just made her really, really happy."

The Australian Government has lifted the ban on the documents same-sex couples need to marry overseas. It has lifted the ban on allowing same-sex couples to marry in foreign consulates in Australia. It is absurd that the Australian Government does not recognise the marriages it now permits. It is cruel that the fulfilment of Lee and Sandra's final wish will not be acknowledged by their own Government.

Judicial appeals

So far I've looked at paths to marriage equality involving legislation. Another path forward is through appeals to courts and tribunals. This is how the reform has progressed in some other countries, particularly Canada and the United States. Unlike them, Australia has no constitutionally guaranteed human rights. An Australian citizen cannot allege to an Australian court that discrimination in the Marriage Act violates their right to equality or right to privacy because the constitution does not guarantee these rights. I am amazed by how many ordinary Australians do not know this. I am approached regularly by people with elaborate plans for High Court challenges based on North American precedents. It is always disappointing to have to disavow them of the rightfully high expectations they have of their own country.

In the absence of a national bill of rights, the Australian Government allows individual citizens to make complaints to the United Nations Human Rights Committee (UNHRC). The key role such complaints have played in the past, for example in the campaign to decriminalise homosexuality in Tasmania or recognise same-sex de facto partners in federal law, leads some same-sex partners to assume it will work again for marriage equality. But there are two big obstacles. The first is that the UNHRC has previously ruled that the human rights enshrined in the International Covenant on Civil and Political Rights do not extend to allowing same-sex marriages. In a marriage equality case from New Zealand in 2006, the Committee found that because the right to marry and have a family explicitly applies to "men" and "women", and not just "people", it only applies to heterosexual couples. The decision has been roundly condemned by human rights experts. When the ICCPR was drafted in the 1960s its reference to matrimony and family life singled out men and women to make it clear that women could make their own choices when it came to marriage, not so homosexuals could be excluded from those choices. Adding weight to this expert criticism are the changes which have occurred since 2006. Many more countries now have marriage equality. The UNHRC has also made decisions on other issues that are inconsistent with its 2006 finding. It is possible a marriage equality case might succeed under the right circumstances. But that still leaves the second big obstacle: implementation. Decisions by the UNHRC are not binding on Australia. The decisions Australia acts on are a tiny minority of those made against it. Common to decisions it has acted on has been the political will to take such action. Unless that will is present it is unlikely a UNHRC decision in favour of marriage equality would lead directly to reform. It would raise the profile of the issue and place it firmly within a human rights framework. But actually changing the law to allow same-sex couples to marry would still lie in the hands of law makers.

While considering judicial appeals I should touch on the issue of the definition of marriage in the Australian Constitution. For many years there was uncertainty about whether "marriage" in that section of the Constitution that allows federal and state governments to make laws for matrimony could encompass same-sex marriages. Originalists argued "no", the Constitution had to be interpreted by standards that applied when the Constitution was proclaimed in 1901. Constructionists argued "yes", because contemporary standards should apply. The High Court resolved this issue in 2013, declaring that the Constitution does allow the federal government to make laws for same-sex marriages. The decision was an important silver lining in the Federal

Government's successful case against the ACT's Marriage Equality Act.

Up until now I've considered possible paths to recognising same-sex marriages in Australia. Now I want to consider two paths that are signposted "marriage equality" but which are far too treacherous to wisely tread.

Civil unions

The first is a proposed path forward that actually isn't, civil unions. I use the term "civil union" to mean any scheme for formally recognising personal relationships through the issue of a certificate, including registered relationships, deeds of relationship and civil partnerships. In Australia a distinction has emerged between registered relationships that are said to recognise existing de facto unions through a dry paper process, and civil unions which are believed to be more like marriage because they include ceremonies and create new legal unions in the same way as a marriage. But in reality this distinction doesn't exist. It was invented by politicians who wanted to appear to support same-sex marriage, or to retreat from that appearance. The state and territory schemes which currently prevail in Australia contain a wide variety of different features that make them more or less like marriage, irrespective of what they are called.

As I discuss in chapter 8, what all civil union schemes have in common is that they do not, and can never, provide full legal equality or dignity for same-sex couples. This is clear from the overseas experience where civil unions have failed to provide same-sex couples with legal equality and security, even when the law says it should. This is because civil unions are not widely understood or respected. It is one thing to have a certificate that you know provides you with key spousal entitlements. It is quite another to convince a figure of authority – an emergency ward doctor or a school principal – who has never seen a civil union certificate before and has no idea what it means. Education about the legal rights associated with civil unions is possible but it cannot even begin to create the same association that exists between love and marriage. Neither can education overcome the fact that giving all same-sex unions a different name reinforces the prejudice that they are somehow different and lesser.

Civil unions can provide couples with an alternative to marriage if that is what they want. In places like France the number of heterosexual couples entering civil unions was many times greater than the number of same-sex couples, even before marriage equality. I support civil unions as an alternative because I believe in personal choice, but I wonder why some social conservatives do. If they genuinely believe the marriage has a unique role as a kind of social glue because of its emphasis on lifelong monogamy, it makes no sense to create another form of recognition with laxer standards. To keep same-sex couples out of marriage, conservative supporters of civil unions create an escape route for different-sex couples. This seems self-defeating and raises questions about their sincerity.

Civil unions can be an alternative to marriage, but they can never be a substitute. This is why most of the countries that have enacted civil union schemes have since moved on to allow same-sex couples to marry. There are people who make the pragmatic case that civil unions are a step towards marriage equality, hastening the latter's eventual achievement by accustoming society to the formal legal recognition of same-sex unions. But there is no evidence for this. The UK and New Zealand had civil unions for a decade before they achieved marriage equality, and for years after marriage equality was achieved in other western countries. This long lag suggests civil unions did more to delay marriage equality than smooth a path to it. Many Australians would find it unacceptable that their LGBTI compatriots would have to wait ten years *after* a future Australia-wide civil union scheme is enacted before they could marry. There is also the question of the federal parliament's power. It cannot make laws for relationships other than marriage unless the states give up their powers to make such laws. The conferral of powers over civil unions would be a long and difficult process. By contrast, marriage equality would be achieved by amending just a few words in the Marriage Act. Instead of going down the civil union path, Australia should learn from the experience in other countries and not repeat their mistake.

A referendum

Another proposal we often hear about from opponents of marriage equality, and a few of its lukewarm supporters, is that it should be decided through a referendum. It's hard to take this proposition seriously when many of the people who say marriage equality is so important the government should spend millions of dollars putting it to the people are also the ones who said it's of so little importance parliament should not waste any time on it (see chapter 9 for more). But I will grant the sincerity of those people of faith who believe marriage is an institution which predates its regulation by government and should therefore not be altered by government. The problem is that the legal definition of marriage has been legislated by parliament many times over hundreds of years. This included the 2004 amendments entrenching marriage as a heterosexual union. Why should the removal of that discrimination be subject to a different process? Why should MPs, who are elected and paid to make decisions like this one, be allowed to abdicate their responsibility?

Such questions are just the start of the case against a referendum. Human rights defenders are rightly concerned about putting inalienable rights to equality and personal autonomy to a show of hands. Constitutional experts ask why a referendum is necessary at all when the High Court made it clear in the ACT marriage equality case that the federal government has the constitutional power to legislate for same-sex marriages. This dispelled previous ambiguity about the issue and removed all possible constitutional questions and hurdles. Given the High Court's decision, a referendum would have to ask Australians whether they want to write a discriminatory definition of marriage into the Constitution, a proposition that would neither advance the issue nor have the slightest chance of success. The reason Ireland had a referendum was because it could not remove its constitutional hurdles to marriage equality without one. Thanks to the High Court decision Australia does not face this problem. When an indicative non-binding plebiscite is proposed instead of a referendum, marriage equality advocates point to the fact that the final decision to change the law would still ultimately lie with parliament, so why spend millions on what would effectively be an elaborate opinion poll?

Opponents of marriage equality aren't shy about explaining why they want a referendum despite all these problems: they believe voters will reject reform. I disagree. The final vote for marriage equality may be lower than opinion polls currently suggest, especially if a referendum is run while one major party opposes change. Some soft supporters of marriage equality, who far outnumber soft opponents for the simple fact that supporters far outnumber opponents, may be persuaded to switch sides by the inevitable fear campaigns. But with public support for marriage equality running at 72% the buffer is large enough to absorb waverers. I have previously seen support for marriage equality dip in the polls when it was voted down in parliament, but it never goes below 55%. This figure represents strong supporters who have been battered by every marriage equality myth and misconception and won't shift, particularly when the end is in sight. I imagine the "yes" vote in a marriage equality referendum would be between around 55% and possibility as high as 60%.

So why do I oppose a national vote? My concern is with the process, not the outcome. I fear that a referendum win may come at too high a price. Here, I'm not just talking about the cost to tax-payers, as well as the cost to non-government organisations that surely have better things to raise money for than the salaries of advertising agents. A referendum campaign would exact a toll on the LGBTI community. US research has shown that the mental health of LGBTI people suffers significantly during referenda debates on marriage equality. When Mark Hatzenbuehler from Columbia University studied tens of thousands of responses to the US National

Institutes of Health's periodic mental health survey, he found that among LGBTI people who experienced a state referendum on marriage equality there was a 37% increase in mood disorders, a 42% increase in alcohol-use disorders, and a 248% increase in generalised anxiety disorders. Remember, this is from a baseline that is already much higher than the general population because of the effects of everyday prejudice. To be sure the referendum was the cause, Hatzenbuehler compared LGBTI people in states with referenda to those in states without. In the latter there was no increase. Referenda are the "X factor", according to Hatzenbuehler. Those he interviewed "… reported multiple stressors during that period. They reported seeing negative media portrayals, anti-gay graffiti. They talked about experiencing a loss of safety and really feeling like these amendments and these policies were really treating them as second-class citizens"[150].

Australian studies about the impact of discriminatory legislation and negative public debate back up these awful US statistics. An analysis by Melbourne clinical psychologist and researcher, Ben Callegari, found a sudden increase in mental health problems among LGBTI Australians after same-sex marriage was banned in 2004. According to his analysis of data collected by the Australian Institute of Health and Welfare there was,

"…a startling and disturbing potential increase in psychiatric illness in Australia following the 2004 amendment to the Marriage Act banning same-sex marriage. It also suggests an improvement in mental health outcomes should same-sex marriage in Australia be allowed into law and a concomitant decrease in economic burden." [151]

A subsequent study by Dr Fiona Barlow from the University of Queensland dug deeper into why this might have been the case. In controlled experiments she exposed same-sex-attracted and different-sex-attracted people to articles in support of and opposed to same-sex marriage. Different-sex attracted participants had a response to the latter which was generally negative. But the response of the same-sex-attracted participants was far worse. They reported feeling depressed, lonely, powerless, hopeless about the future, failed in life and more fearful of assault. The researchers concluded,

"...that opposition to same-sex marriage has a direct, immediate, and negative effect on the health and wellbeing of the people to whom marriage is denied. If we extrapolate from our current results, it is possible that the Government's current stance on same-sex marriage may have a marked and harmful effect on the health and happiness of sexual minority individuals at large." [152]

As dramatic as these statistical and experimental findings are, they come as no surprise to anyone involved in LGBTI human rights campaigns. In the 1990s in Tasmania the debate on decriminalising homosexuality was in the news every day, more often than not because of the hateful statements of public figures. Many LGBTI people left Tasmania to escape this constant and often ugly public discussion about their lives. It drove some to take their own lives, including Nick Donovan, a young man in Northern Tasmania. Nick could no longer handle the hate and had bought a plane ticket out. But neither could he bring himself to leave his home. The night before he was due to leave he killed himself. We know the pressures Nick was under because he left a note explaining them. Many others driven to their grave by Tasmania's obsessive debate kept the reason to themselves out of fear or shame. How much more pressure would be felt by today's young LGBTI people during a national referendum where every nasty old myth and stereotype is likely to find a public figure to voice it? A referendum would cost too many lives. Of that, I have no doubt. A path to marriage equality strewn with the bodies of dead young Australians is not a path anyone with a sympathetic heart wants to walk down.

Doing nothing at all

The final path to marriage equality I should address is the one of least resistance, but also the one least likely to succeed. There is a perception in the community that marriage equality is inevitable, and we should just sit back and wait for it. It's true that history's arc bends towards marriage equality as I've outlined in chapter 11. It's also true the argument for the inevitability of marriage equality has been a useful response to those who declare it cannot or should not ever occur. But sometimes the perception of inevitability backfires. It can create a sense of complacency. Not a few times have I heard supporters and sceptics alike declare "marriage equality is going to happen whatever we do or don't do". My response is that history is only a name for our collective actions as individuals. It has no other motor driving it this way or that. If we choose not to act, we forfeit our claim on the future and history will be bent away from marriage equality.

Why are some paths better than others?

Each different path to marriage equality raises its own hopes and conceals its own pitfalls. But in my mind there is a clear distinction. I favour those paths forward that immediately allow marriage to take place or existing marriages to be recognised. The paths that promise this, only after some great hurdle is jumped or long time elapsed, should be treated with deep suspicion. This is because same-sex couples marrying will be immensely important to the couples and families concerned. It will also help assuage lingering fears in parts of the Australian community. But most of all it is because a goal deferred is a goal more easily defeated.

13. What can you do?

Australia has conducted and concluded its debate on marriage equality. Polls show support is at 72%, higher than many countries with marriage equality. There is majority support in every demographic including rural, older and religious Australians. Strong opposition is only 14%. To put that figure in perspective, 22% of Australians are regular church-goers. Even among those people who have been deemed irrevocably opposed to marriage equality many have come around.

The task before marriage equality supporters is less to increase support for reform than to ensure existing support is heard by politicians. Too many law-makers only hear the unfounded fears and anxieties of the tiny minority against marriage equality. Among the broad range of marriage equality supporters who show up in opinion polls there are too few who speak out. Fortunately, there are ways to reverse this situation.

Organisations campaigning for marriage equality present supporters with a welter of ways they can express their support. They are encouraged to sign petitions, attend rallies or share posts on Facebook. Such activities, if well targeted, can inform others, raise the profile of the issue and boost the morale of existing supporters. But they can fall short of bringing new law makers into the marriage equality fold. Nothing transforms attitudes on key social issues like interpersonal contact. For example, Australian polling shows people who know same-sex partners are much more likely to support marriage equality. For example, research by Crosby/Texter found 76% support for marriage equality among Australians who know someone who is gay, compared to 50% support among those who don't[153]. It would seem that familiarity breeds respect.

We can see the same dramatic impact of interpersonal contact on Australian politicians. The most prominent Australian politician to change his mind on marriage equality was Kevin Rudd. When he announced his support for the reform in May 2013 he explained it was triggered by a conversation with a former staffer and evangelical Christian who was also gay[154]. More recently, Liberal MP, Josh Frydenberg, has attributed his change of heart to the personal stories he heard from his constituents, including one female couple. In his words "the meeting ended in tears and that did have an effect on me"[155].

The first challenge facing members of the marriage equality movement is to find ways to have these conversations with local politicians, and with lukewarm and silent supporters of the reform. Some politicians will try to avoid what they believe is a difficult issue. Some are reluctant to meet, or just don't respond to requests. The national spokesperson for Parents and Friends of Lesbians and Gays, Shelley Argent, has some useful advice for such situations. She suggests by-passing the politician's minders. Instead, phone their office and ask to speak directly to the diary secretary. Also, team up with other people in the electorate and go in a group. This will make it harder to knock you back.

Reaching out to uninvolved supporters to encourage them to speak up can be just as difficult. But local marriage equality groups have been established with this aim in mind. Starting in Tasmania in 2012 with successful family BBQs, these groups have sprung up across suburban, regional and rural Australia. They have convened town hall meetings, conducted marriage equality film nights and held street stalls. At such stalls members of the public are encouraged to sign postcards that are later collected together and sent to MPs, but no less important are the conversations that ensue.

Sharyn Faulkner from Geelong writes about what her group has achieved:

"Geelong for Marriage Equality was convened in 2014. A group of people met with Sarah Henderson, Liberal MP for Corangamite, she challenged us to prove to her that people wanted Marriage Equality. We held stalls at various locations and obtained over 2,000 signed postcards which were hand delivered. We set up a Facebook Page with nearly 1300 likes and encouraged those people to write to her. I wrote to the Geelong Football Club and they put an open letter on their webpage supporting marriage equality. I then wrote to the AFL CEO, Gillon McLaughlin, who also wrote a letter supporting marriage equality. This was reported worldwide. I approached The City of Greater Geelong and Surf Coast Shire to write to Sarah and show their support for marriage equality. We have encouraged several same-sex couples to tell their stories in the Geelong Advertiser to keep the momentum going. We organised a local screening of "The Case Against 8" with Human Rights Commissioner, Tim Wilson, speaking beforehand. We also have the support of the Queenscliffe/Pt Lonsdale Uniting Church and their Ministers have been very outspoken on the issue. When Sarah had open offices at

various locations around the electorate we have made sure that we have had people there to speak to her in person about marriage equality. However, the campaign continues and we will not give up until marriage equality is passed."

As Sharyn highlights, a particularly valuable feature of the work of local groups has been mustering support from local sports teams, churches and councils. Not only have these community groups and representatives publicly expressed their support for marriage equality, they have written directly to local MPs about it. In some parts of the country, marriage equality groups have even begun door-to-door canvassing, an initiative I hope will spread. But you don't have to wear your soles out to encourage others to take action. Neither do you need to be a part of a larger group. For example, it is increasingly common for heterosexual couples to make a point at their wedding about the exclusion of their LGBTI friends and relatives from marriage, and to encourage those present to do something about it. Whatever you do, the point is to encourage less likely local supporters of reform to raise their voice; people of faith, older people, sports people, socially conservative people, people who have changed their minds, people who are from the same background as the local MP, whoever makes the best influencer.

The importance of personal story telling

The next challenge for marriage equality campaigners, once they have the willing ear of their local MP or fellow community member, is to decide what to say. Most Australians will have heard statements about equality, fairness and discrimination before. What they may not have heard is your individual story about why marriage equality is important to you and those around you.

Research into how and why people change their minds on marriage equality has found personal stories make all the difference[156]. This shouldn't be a surprise. Neurologists have discovered that being told about an experience in narrative form affects the brain as if we have lived that experience. Evolutionary biologists argue humans evolved to tell stories to foster social empathy and bonding necessary for survival[157]. Whatever lies behind the power of personal stories, they are immensely effective in showing how marriage inequality affects ordinary people day-to-day. They tap into our desire to understand the ideas and feelings of others.

Some people say they have no story to tell, but I have never found anyone who was truly bereft. A grandmother at an Australian Marriage Equality workshop in Adelaide complained to me: "I have a gay grandson who is a lawyer. He is highly respected in his field and does lots of pro bono work for Aboriginal people, but there's no story in that". "The story", I told her, "is that your son contributes his all to the law, but in return it treats him as second-class". Some people have a story that others wrongly discount. In 2012 Australian Marriage Equality brought together marriage equality supporters from across Australia to Parliament House to lobby representatives from their states. I took charge of the Tasmanian contingent. In a meeting with one sceptical Liberal Senator I assumed the young, lesbian couple from his home district, who contribute immensely to their local community, would make the biggest splash. In fact, it was the older transgender person from Hobart whose story I included in chapter 2. She talked about being married when she was a man, how that marriage ended when her wife drowned, and how she has since undergone gender reassignment. She talked about being in another equally committed relationship today, also with a woman. "I am still the same person. My current relationship is as committed and meaningful as my former marriage. Why could I marry then and not now?" she asked the Senator. Unexpectedly, this spoke directly to his understanding of marriage as a fundamentally gendered institution. He said he had never before seen the issue as the transgender person saw it, and he could no longer justify his stance in the way he had.

Some elements of good personal story telling

It is impossible to know which personal story will tip another person into supporting marriage equality. But what we do know is that there are ways of telling stories more effectively. Melbourne corporate trainer and marriage equality advocate, Shawn Callahan, has some very useful tips.

"A personal story has the best chance of influencing a political decision. The problem is that many people don't really understand how to tell their story. To be meaningful, the story should be about something unexpected that happened that we care about. It's a personal story if it happened to you. Here is a simple example from my own life:

"A couple of years ago, my daughter told me and her mother that she was gay. We told her we loved her no matter what. But it did get us thinking that she would have a harder life than many others because of the prejudice and inequality in Australia."

"As you can see, while this is a story, it's not the most compelling story. The best stories in support of marriage equality have a clear point, are visual in that you can see the action happening in your mind's eye, and convey emotion. Let me rework the story concerning my daughter with the above principles in mind:

"Ever since my daughter Alex moved into a group house, she has come back to our house on Monday nights for a home-cooked meal. On one of these Monday nights, I arrived home to find my wife Sheenagh and Alex in the kitchen, clearly in the midst of talking about something important. 'Go on, tell Dad', Sheenagh said. Alex then told me she was gay. We immediately hugged, and I told her how much Sheenagh and I loved her and how we would support her no matter what. Later that night, after Alex had gone home, Sheenagh started crying. When I asked her what was upsetting her, she said she was worried about the harder life Alex would face because of the prejudice and inequality that same-sex couples had to confront. You can now see why we think marriage equality is so important."

"The first thing to notice is that I included names in my story. It makes the story feel real. Even if you can't use real names because of privacy concerns, it's still worth referring to pseudonyms. Just say something like, 'A couple of months ago, Marie (not her real name) ...'"

"Did you see us standing in our kitchen? Did you see Alex and I hug? What about Sheenagh crying? Did these moments make you feel anything? Did you get a sense of how we felt?

If you did, you'll better understand the simple point I was trying to make with this story: Why should our sons and daughters face a harder life just because of prejudice against *them and the person they simply love and want to marry? It just doesn't make sense in a country like Australia that prides itself on a fair go for everyone."*

In this book I deliberately selected quotes from people who tell their stories well. Here's four extracts from narratives that can be found elsewhere in this book. After each, I explain what they illustrate about good personal story telling.

"It is very sad, that in this day and age in Australia, the land of the 'fair go', there is still a group of citizens like us, who have to regularly log on to Google and devote significant chunks of time to working out what our rights are in different parts of Australia."

What I liked about this quote from Davina Storer is the use of a simple, universal image – "googling" – to illustrate the point that same-sex relationship rights are patchy and marriage is a solution to this. Many heterosexual people find it hard to grasp this because they take their rights, and the universal recognition of these rights, for granted.

"I listened to the arguments that said that the state could legally recognise same-sex relationships but not call it 'marriage'. In the end it began to sound snobby. It began to sound as though the underlying message was 'Please don't let them into our exclusive club. Please reserve this badge of honour for our group only, and exclude them'."

I chose this quote from Baptist Pastor, Nathan Nettleton, because of the use of the word "snobby". It perfectly encapsulates the condescending attitude to same-sex relationships that too often relegates us to second-class status. Sometimes LGBTI people are wary of using value-laden terms because so many such terms have been used against us. But, used sparingly, they can be immensely powerful. The other obvious merit in the above quote is that it is from someone who, at first appearance, is an unlikely supporter of marriage equality. However, upon reflection it's clearer how his concern about exclusion is consistent with his religious background.

"One (Aboriginal) student pointed out the similarities between interracial marriage and same-sex marriage. She turned to me and said, "What's the big deal? When will they ever learn???" She was visibly upset and frustrated that the government could not see the simple truth that she could."

Telling the stories of those people around you, especially those who cannot speak publicly themselves, can be very effective. I chose this quote, from teacher Kim Burman, because it links the experience of two different minorities over time, and because the direct and unaffected voice of a child is magnified in a credible way through the re-telling of her teacher.

"I have been in a happy relationship for 38 years. My partner and I were both migrants arriving to Australia in the '50s. He was German and I was Jewish who not so long before spent my childhood and adolescence in a concentration camp. Yet we overcame a great obstacle because we have found love was stronger than hate. We built our lives, together. We brought family to Australia, who in turn prospered and had families of their own. We lived in the same house we bought and had a wonderful relationship with our neighbours and people at large. Our foundation was solid."

This quote from Holocaust survivor, Frank Weisinger, is my favourite passage in the whole book. What I find most compelling about it is that an aspect of Frederick's personal story – the unlikely but successful match of a Holocaust survivor and a non-Jewish German – illustrates that marriage is about love not hate, bridges, not boundaries. The story also illustrates that same-sex partners are not only part of families, but can play a pivotal part in their families' destiny. This effectively highlights the absurdity of excluding same-sex partners from marriage on the basis of "family values".

The national story

As we've seen, every individual has their own story to tell about marriage equality. When these stories are told, those listening get a stronger sense of the personhood of the story teller and can empathise with them more. But the stories we tell about marriage equality shouldn't be limited to our own individual lives. The action groups I have already mentioned have begun to tell a marriage equality story that is about place. Their story can be about a post-industrial community re-inventing itself as more creative and inclusive. It can be about a stable and long-established community living up to its promise of hospitality, respect and belonging for all. It can be an economically dynamic community reaching out to skilled and innovative people regardless of their background. Whatever the local story may be, locating marriage equality in a particular place is key to making it less abstract and more relevant to many people.

Local marriage equality narratives may also be the key to finally constructing what has been all-too-often absent from the Australian marriage equality debate, an optimistic national narrative. There have been national narratives about how backward and intolerant Australia has become, or how weak or malign this or that government was. But they do nothing other than assuage frustration and confirm conceit. They certainly do nothing to inspire supporters of reform to take action. Only a positive national narrative about how marriage equality is a milestone in Australia's historical progress towards fulfilling its promise of legal and social equity will inspire supporters in sufficient numbers to finally overcome the recalcitrance of politicians. Whoever tells this story so the nation hears, will have contributed as much as anyone can to the achievement of marriage equality.

For more on how you can become part of the movement for marriage equality visit the Australian Marriage Equality website: www.australianmarriageequality.org

DIGRESSIONS FROM THE

AUSTRALIAN MARRIAGE

EQUALITY DEBATE

Introduction to section three

I have labeled the following three essays "digressions" because it is not their primary purpose to make the case for marriage equality. They contain reflections on why marriage equality is important. But these are incidental to the wider issues they address.

The first essay is an overview of freedom to marry in Australian history: why this freedom was violated, how it was won back, and how this has propelled Australian society forward. The second, examines the case against marriage equality from the left and reflects on the relationship between marriage equality and changing ideas about what it means to be gay. This essay is a counterweight to the case I make in the first section of the book addressing the conservative case against marriage equality. It also speaks to what are, for me, fundamental issues of personal identity and political purpose. The third essay does the same. It looks at the campaign for marriage equality in Tasmania as a way of understanding what it means to be Tasmanian and changing attitudes towards the Island.

In their own way each essay contributes to the national narrative about marriage equality I referred to in the last chapter. But they are only slivers of that story and not meant to complete the picture.

Two of these essays – the first and third – were originally published elsewhere. They deal in a more detailed way with some of the ideas already dealt with in sections one and two of this book. I have tried my best to limit repetition.

14. 'True and good citizens': a history of freedom to marry in Australia

A version of this essay was published in Overland, Winter *2011*

'Moral terrorists'

On Friday August 13th 2004, in an unusually emotional debate punctuated by tears and rage, the Australian Senate passed a Howard Government amendment to the national Marriage Act defining matrimony as the exclusive union between one man and one woman for life.

That had been the definition ascribed to marriage by the courts for over a century, one law-makers felt too obvious to declare in statute. But then Canadian provinces began solemnising same-sex marriages, starting with Ontario in 2003. Because there is no residency requirement for marriage in Canada, a steady stream of Australian same-sex couples flowed across the Pacific to wed, only to have their marital rights effectively taken away from them when they returned to Australia.

At the beginning of 2004 two such couples sought a ruling from the Federal Court on whether Australia's relatively liberal laws on the recognition of foreign marriages might extend to the recognition of their Canadian unions. The court was never allowed to offer its view. Liberal Senator, Guy Barnett, petitioned the Prime Minister to "protect marriage" from being "demeaned and degraded". The petition was successful, not least because it was an election year in both Australia and the US. In America the politicisation of "gay marriage" was proving useful in welding wealthy and highly-disciplined evangelical churches to the Republican Party. Australian conservatives hoped for the same result here. The Howard Government's marriage amendment – declaring matrimony to be exclusively heterosexual and removing the powers of the courts to recognise overseas same-sex unions - was raced through Parliament shoving aside Government anti-terror legislation.

For good measure, the Prime Minister addressed a rowdy meeting in the Great Hall of Parliament House in defence of "traditional marriage" during which homosexuals were condemned as "moral terrorists". In the corridors outside, in protests around the nation and in thousands of submissions to a concurrent Senate inquiry into Howard's amendments, supporters of same-sex marriage pleaded that this was a matter of legal equality and anti-discrimination. But neither major party was listening. In her address to the anti-gay audience in the Great Hall, then Shadow Attorney-General, Nicola Roxon, declared Labor's support for entrenching discrimination against same-sex relationships. She was given a standing ovation[158].

The events of 2004 have defined the debate on same-sex marriage ever since. Religious groups continue to have disproportionate influence over the policies of both major parties. Supporters of reform continue to make the case that equality and anti-discrimination are the primary principles at stake. The far more intense American debate on same-sex marriage inevitably influences and overshadows its Australian equivalent.

But there is another way of understanding the Australian ban on same-sex marriage and the subsequent campaign to have this ban overturned, one which puts the issue in a longer-term and thoroughly Australian context. As well as entrenching legal inequality and discrimination, the 2004 Marriage Act amendment was an assault on the freedom of Australian citizens to marry the person of their choice. Australians in same-sex relationships still have the notional right to marry, but that right is absurdly curtailed to members of the other sex. Not one of us has the freedom to marry the person who we most wish to marry, our same-sex partner. When we see the ban on same-sex marriage as a negation by overbearing governments of the freedom to marry it takes its place in a long list of similar restrictions that have been imposed on Australians for over two hundred years. These restrictions created personal distress and clearly breached the human dignity of those concerned. But they had something more in common. They were devised by governments so arrogant they assumed they had the authority to tell individual Australians who they could and couldn't marry. They were imposed as part, often a pivotal part, of great, flawed visions to re-shape Australian society. Defiance of restrictions on the freedom to marry, and the eventual removal of these restrictions, have been equally pivotal in overturning the repressive ideologies imposed on ordinary Australians. Indeed, freedom to marry has helped define and propel some of the greatest emancipation movements in our history, transforming not just the lives of those denied this freedom, but the society eventually convinced to grant it.

'She only married to be free'

For the half century after 1788 colonial governments decided who, how and when the majority of Australians married. The fact that convicts had to apply to the authorities for permission to marry the partner of their choice was an important symbol that they had forfeited control over their own lives and were no longer full citizens. More than this, the fact convicts were not free to marry was used and abused by the convict authorities for particular policy ends, usually to deal with perceived social problems, often to implement a certain social vision, always to maintain social control.

Australia's first viceroy, Arthur Phillip, was one of the last representatives of a class of eighteenth century administrators who believed public policy could buttress the agrarian class system industrialism was soon to overwhelm. His vision of transforming boatloads of British felons into a native Australian yeomanry hinged on rewarding male convicts who married with free time and small parcels of land so that they might establish their own acred households[159].

Later governors like Darling and Arthur embraced the changes Phillip hoped to halt. Their policy was to inculcate their charges with values of the new industrial middle class: hard work, self control and a strictly gendered division of labour. The definition of a good husband shifted from physically strong to skilled and sober, of a wife from chaste and virtuous to useful and industrious[160]. Convicts who conformed were encouraged to marry. Those who resisted were forbidden[161].

To achieve their goals, Australia's colonial authorities more closely regulated working class marriages than ever before and certainly more than they were regulated in Britain. The dislocation of colonial life also increased official oversight of who married, when and why. In Australia, the traditional roles played by extended family, established local communities and clergy in negotiating and sealing marriage were assumed by the state. In 1839 the government of Van Diemen's Land, the Australian colony with the highest proportion of convicts, was the first to take over the church's traditional role of issuing marriage certificates. Not for the last time, some clerics found a new role advocating, Friar Lawrence-like, for couples whose applications for government permission to marry were denied[162].

In none of this did the authorities show much interest in respecting or enhancing marriage as it was generally understood. In the rush to have particular convicts marry, the likelihood of bigamy was sometimes ignored and the possibility of a clash of faiths over-looked. Romantic love, religious duty, personal financial security, or the legitimisation of sex and children were not considered valid reasons for granting permission to marry. For example, pregnancy was rarely grounds for granting the marriage application of a female convict, although some women seeking permission proffered it as one[163]. The desire for respectability was also not a common reason for permission to marry, permission being granted more as a reward for "reformation" than a means to it[164]. The authorities even sometimes turned a blind eye to unmarried cohabitation because any heterosexual relationships were better than none. For early Australian authorities the ideological purposes they imposed on marriage through their manipulation of permission to marry took precedence over any of the ends marriage is more commonly associated with.

Ironically, it was sometimes the convicts themselves who showed a greater respect for the traditional, cultural associations of marriage. Deep-seated affection most adequately explains repeated applications from couples repeatedly refused. A desire to legitimise offspring through marriage explains repeated applications from partners expecting children. Of course, many sought to marry for more pragmatic, economic reasons, as did their social peers in Britain at the time. Indeed, marriage rates were sometimes higher in Australia[165], suggesting those who suffered the mass social dislocation and arbitrary abuses of convict Australia sought security, certainty and steadiness in marriage. We can also see a degree of pragmatism in the way many convicts tailored their marriage applications to highlight the middle-class virtues the authorities wanted to reward. But it would be wrong to consider the reasons convicts wanted to marry to be as uniformly unsentimental and impersonal as the reasons they were, or were not, allowed to wed.

The one constant in the twists and turns of convict marriage policy was that matrimony was considered by the authorities the best way to control female convicts by handing authority over them from the state to their husbands. But not all women saw it this way. Some used marriage to escape particular employers, others, to find some level of financial independence in what was for them "a seller's market"[166]. Many used wedlock to escape the convict system altogether, sometimes with the collusion of their male partner[167]. Intent on exercising the freedom from convict discipline she believed marriage bestowed, Mary Furner explained, "I am kept in bondage...(until I marry); I shall then be enabled to become in a manner of speaking a free subject"[168]. Penelope Burke was more succinct, stating to the authorities that she "only married to be free"[169]. According to witnesses to the Bigge Commission she was not alone. "Female convicts often married only to alter their civil status", Bigge reported, giving this his conditional approval as the lesser of two evils[170].

Of course, marriage for some convict women was just another form of bondage. Some husbands mistreated their convict wives. Some husbands disappeared back into the convict system effectively abandoning their spouse. Some even recommitted their wives to that system. But for a significant number of early European Australians, marriage was a site of both legal and personal freedom, as much as it was another symbol of servitude for others. Indeed the more overbearingly it was regulated and put to ends beyond itself, the more opportunities it seemed to offer for the rarest commodity in convict Australia, personal autonomy.

For campaigners against convict transportation the principle of freedom to marry was also important in their struggle for personal liberty and against governmental intervention. Modelling themselves on the American anti-slavery movement, opponents of convictism maintained that a society's prosperity and stability depended on the right of all to make contracts - political, commercial and matrimonial – free of compulsion. At the rhetorical edge of this emancipatory theory was the fear and loathing anti-transportationists whipped up against homosexuality in Australia's gaols. Free of official oversight and regulation, it was argued, men and women would follow their natural inclinations into happy fruitful wedlock and away from sexual vice.

Albeit on the back of homophobia, the principle of freedom to marry helped propel anti-transportationists to their victory over convictism, a victory that sparked local movements for democracy and nationalism. Colonial governments stepped back from their strict, day-to-day supervision of marriage, as they did from the grand penological experiments marriage had been crucial to carrying out.

But the tyranny freedom to marry dethroned in the public sphere took much longer to overturn within marriage itself. Whatever opportunities to improve their legal status the old-style of marriage regulation had given some female convicts now evaporated. Upon wedding, women ceased to be not only equal citizens but individuals with human dignity, becoming instead the near property of their husbands, their personhoods subsumed.

In the Twentieth Century, even when women no longer suffered these indignities, married women had to fight, again mostly with the authorities, to remove strict state restrictions over abortion, contraception and divorce. The Government's meddling took away their right to decide when and who they married, how they conducted their marriages, and how these marriages might end. For women seeking to improve their legal and social status, reform of laws about marriage and married life was about pushing back state intrusion, assuming greater control over their lives, asserting their equal citizenship and obtaining some degree of self-determination, freedom and choice.

Other, much less visible groups of Australians shared that struggle. Of the occupying powers in post-war Japan only two, the United States and Australia, refused to sanction or recognise the marriages of their troops to Japanese civilians. In a premonition of Australia's contemporary marriage debates, some diggers with Japanese fiancés married in the Canadian embassy and, denied the right to return to Australia with their new spouses, ended their tour of duty in the country that had married them. Not until 1964, with the unravelling of the White Australia Policy, would the law of their nation of origin recognise their partner of choice[171].

Not only were interracial marriages adversely impacted by the White Australia Policy, they also contributed directly to dismantling it. The most famous example was the marriage of John O'Keefe to Annie Maas Jacob, an Indonesian who had been granted temporary asylum in Australia during World War Two. Despite their marriage, the Calwell Labor Government sought to forcibly repatriate Annie and her children in 1949. In response, the family mounted a High Court challenge which they won. The O'Keefe family had strong support, including from the then Archbishop of Melbourne, Daniel Mannix. Many supporters stressed the sanctity of marriage. In a letter to the Prime Minister, Doreen Riley declared he was wrecking a marriage that 'no man can put asunder'[172].

Calwell was unhappy with the High Court ruling. In his words, "the High Court decision in the O'Keefe case goes far beyond the question of repatriation of a single Indonesian family. It knocks down the pillars upon which the White Australia Policy has firmly rested"[173]. He planned to pass overriding legislation but his opportunity was lost with Labor's election defeat. The incoming Liberal Government of Robert Menzies let the ruling stand. John and Annie O'Keefe's mutual love and devotion had trumped the racism that had underpinned Australian immigration policy for decades.

Beyond convicts, women, overseas servicemen and migrants there is another group of Australians to whom the right to marry freely is even more central to their story, to their subjection, to their freedom and to their demands for respect. Like the convicts, their right to marry the partner of their choice was denied in the name of a greater good. Like women, their struggle to defend that right became central to their emancipation. Like servicemen and migrants, the achievement of that right was part of a broader transformation in Australian society.

'We ask for our Freedom so that we can rule our lives'

On August 13th 1959, exactly 45 years to the day before Federal Parliament amended the Marriage Act to prohibit any recognition of same-sex marriages, debate on the Bill that would become that Act - Australia's first national marriage law - was interrupted by a question about a controversial legal battle unfolding in the Northern Territory. In what was destined to be the most publicised case of its kind, a young black woman, Gladys Namagu, had been denied permission to marry her fiancé, a white drover named Mick Daly, by the Protector of Aborigines in Darwin[174].

Like his counterparts in Queensland and Western Australia, the Northern Territory Protector controlled every aspect of the lives of Aboriginal people, including who they married. Government control over Indigenous marriage stretched back to the 1860s when the Victorian Government passed laws allowing it to expel Aborigines from their reserves if they married across racial lines, ostensibly to reduce the numbers claiming government assistance[175]. Fears of racial contamination were more clearly the motive behind the passage of the first law assuming direct control over marriages involving Indigenous people in Queensland in 1897[176]. As federation channelled and heightened white Australia's fears for its racial integrity, Western Australia and the Northern Territory followed Queenland's example (South Australia passed an Aboriginal marriage law for the Territory it then governed but not for itself. Like NSW and Victoria it felt its Aboriginal problem would soon be solved by extinction[177]). Beginning as a control on the marriage of black women to white or Asian men, these laws grew steadily in scope and ever more strict in their enforcement, until, at their peak in the 1930s, they regulated the marriages of all Aboriginal people of all ancestries to all other people and to each other.

As these laws grew more intrusive, so they also began to be employed, like the marriage controls endured by convicts, to implement official ideologies. These ideologies often diverged dramatically between the Australian states, even though the laws behind them were remarkably consistent. In Queensland, the Chief Protector generally used his power over Aboriginal marriages to bar the unions of whites with Aborigines of both full and mixed descent. This was based on the belief that Europeans and Aborigines were at either end of the racial ladder, and their unions inevitably disruptive of the social order and damaging for the resulting children. Concern was not infrequently expressed that mixed race children combined the worst features of their parents' races, were physically and mentally weaker and more prone to alcoholism, sexual aberration and Communism[178].

On the other side of the continent, Western Australia's Chief Protector, A.O Neville held what he believed to be the more modern view that Aborigines were second only to Europeans in the racial hierarchy. Because whites and blacks were racial kin the latter could be quickly absorbed by interbreeding with the former without the risk of throw-backs or degeneration. As the ultimate guarantee of a white Australia, interracial unions were to be encouraged, and same-race marriages between Aborigines, especially those of mixed-descent, forbidden[179].

Reflecting its geography, the Northern Territory fell between Queensland and WA ideologically. First it adopted Queensland's policy of barring interracial marriages. Later it adopted WA's policy of using marriage controls for the opposite ends of barring same-race unions. By the time of Mick and Gladys, federal governance of the Territory meant unmarried young women like Gladys were considered state wards with their applications to marry judged case-by-case.

As racial ideology drove ever greater intrusion into the marriage choices of Aboriginal people, so Aboriginal people found ways to appeal, dodge or dissent from this intrusion. The meticulous record keeping of the WA Protector's office reveals a steady increase in the number of appeals against marriage denials, from Aboriginal men and women often guided through the bureaucratic maze by mission priests. Like their forebears in convict times, some mission clergy were champions of the freedom of Aboriginal people to marry because in their eyes marriage was a contract between two willing partners and God, and not properly a tool of secular social engineering. Given the protectors showed as little regard as earlier convict authorities for the traditional reasons for marriage - love, sex, children, personal stability, financial security and/or religious faith - the convergent role of penal ministers and mission priests should come as no surprise. Nor should it be a surprise that for Aborigines enduring the breakdown of kinship networks, social dislocation and all the arbitrary abuses inflicted on a subject people, marriage and the security it promised was just as important as it had been to convicts in a similar situation a century before.

After repeated denials, some Aborigines took matters into their own hands. Like many of her peers in the same frustrating predicament, and like many convict women before her, one young West Australian woman's simple solution was pregnancy.

"This is the second time I've asked for permission to marry my boy", she declared to the Matron of Moore River Settlement in 1934.

"I know what to do. I will go to the settlement and I'll have a cause." [180]

Unfortunately that wasn't always enough. Having married across the wrong race divide, Jack and Lallie Akbar had to flee from Western Australia to South Australia to escape prosecution[181]. Having married across the right one Jessie Smith incurred Neville's wrath for continuing to play an active part in Aboriginal community life and thereby refusing to assimilate[182].

Western Australia was also the site of some of the first organised protests against marriage control. The 1935 petition from "half-caste" women in Broome that I cited in chapter 1, echoed the aspirations of convict women a century earlier by couching freedom to marry in terms of social advancement.

"Sometimes we have the chance to marry a man of our own choice. Who may be in better circumstances than ourselves.... therefore we ask for our Freedom so that when the chance comes along we can rule our lives and make ourselves true and good citizens." [183]

Over east, the Aboriginal rights movement that began in the 1920s was slow to pick up the demand for the freedom to marry. It had grown out of the labour movement, was dominated by men and focused its energies on wages and conditions. The pain of marriage laws was felt a long way from its base in Sydney and Melbourne. So far away, in fact, that no mention is made of freedom to marry in the manifestos of the Australian Aboriginal Progressive Association or the Australian Aborigines League until the late 1930s when it suddenly jumps to near the top of their list of demands. In the Ten Point plan for Aboriginal people resolved by the national conference called in 1938 to mourn the 150th anniversary of white invasion and subsequently presented to Prime Minister Lyons, freedom to marry is rated above every other violation of Aboriginal civil rights bar unequal pay and access to pensions.

"We recommend that Aborigines and Halfcastes should come under the same marriage laws as white people, and should be free to marry partners of their choice, irrespective of colour." [184]

The expanded scope and stricter implementation of laws governing Aboriginal marriage in WA, Queensland and the Northern Territory in the mid 1930s, and the advent of local voices raised against these developments, may explain why marriage was now on the national Aboriginal agenda. What explains its high priority was the link Aboriginal activists sort to make between Australia's race laws and those of Australia's emerging new enemy, Nazi Germany. The pamphlets that, for the first time, highlighted Australia's racially-based marriage laws, were also for the first time peppered with references to "Hitlerism". Advocates clearly hoped white Australians repulsed by the Nuremberg Laws would see how similar laws in their own country were a cornerstone for a similar rotten, racist edifice [185].

Eventually white Australians did make this connection but not simply because, and certainly not immediately after, they fought and helped defeat Nazism. In post-war Australia the campaign for Indigenous rights continued to be driven by those ordinary Aborigines prepared to protest the denial of their freedom to marry and by those activists who kept the issue before decision-makers. But now they had a much greater ally, the entrenchment of human rights in international treaties, increased public discussion and understanding of what these rights meant, and the development around these rights of a canon of serious thought. In chapter 1 I cited the words of political theorist Hannah Arendt who, in 1959, explained the link between human rights and freedom to marry. It's worth revisiting what she said:

"The right to marry whoever one wishes is an elementary human right compared to which 'the right to attend an integrated school, the right to sit where one pleases on a bus, regardless of one's skin color or race' are minor indeed. Even political rights, like the right to vote...are secondary".

All these elements coalesced in the case of Gladys and Mick. When news of their plight broke in 1959 it made headlines nationally. They were dubbed an outback Romeo and Juliet. The outpouring of public sympathy was overwhelming. On the back of this sympathy, meetings in defence of Gladys and Mick were convened around the country. A case was even mounted to the Secretary-General of the United Nations. When the matter was raised in Federal Parliament in August 1959, MPs demanded and received an assurance from the Government that discrimination would never be written into the landmark national marriage legislation they were poised to pass. Thanks to this public focus, within a few short months the prohibition on Gladys and Mick's marriage had been lifted and the power to impose such prohibitions removed.

But more than this, the case of Gladys and Mick, like the notorious mistreatment of Aboriginal artist, Albert

Namatjira, pricked the national conscience and led directly to the dismantling over the next few years, of the whole elaborate and awful system of Aboriginal protection laws that had prevailed in Australia for a hundred years.

It was no coincidence that when activists listed the aspirations of Indigenous people during the 1967 referendum campaign on full Aboriginal citizenship, the right to marry the person of one's choice was still at the top of the list, above the right to custody of their children and access to traditional lands, and second only to the right to vote.

It is a source of great pride for many contemporary Australians that the 1967 referendum was endorsed by 91% of Australian voters, most of whom, of course, were white. But what many white Australians have forgotten is that this important moment in our national history was made possible, in part, by the importance so many Australians placed on the freedom to marry.

'Turning back the clock 140 years'

We have seen that the history of freedom to marry in Australia is the history of flawed plans to manipulate society by controlling who ordinary people wed, of the defiance of these plans by those who would make this choice themselves, and of the evolution of Australian society this defiance sparked.

The most recent example of this old pattern is the violation of the right of lesbian, gay, bisexual, transgender and intersex (LGBTI) people to freely marry the partner of their choice. Like its predecessors, the 2004 same-sex marriage ban became the legal principle upon which an elaborate edifice of discriminatory law and policy-making was founded. This edifice sprawled well beyond gays, marriage, federal law and even Australia. Like its predecessors, today's denial of the freedom to marry became part of establishing a larger and oppressive social vision. Challenging and dismantling this edifice and these ideologies has had implications far beyond the legal rights of same-sex couples.

In federal law, the 2004 ban on same-sex marriage was repeatedly cited to deny same-sex couples recognition in other areas. It was the excuse the Howard Government gave when it denied same-sex couples the federal entitlements available to opposite-sex de facto spouses. The Government ignored calls from the Australian Human Rights Commission, the UN Human Rights Committee and its own backbenchers to allow same-sex couples relationship entitlements as de facto partners, repeatedly arguing that de facto marriages are a type of marriage and same-sex marriage is not allowed. When it did recognise same-sex partners, in limited areas like defence force entitlements and superannuation, it labelled them companion-like "interdependents" to underline its determination to keep the idea of gay conjugality out of national law. Under the first Rudd Government de facto status was granted to same-sex couples but only after immense intellectual effort went into severing the concept from marriage, again on the pretext that the 2004 same-sex marriage ban made this necessary. Giving de facto status to same-sex couples was portrayed as providing them with "practical day-to-day financial and workplace and entitlements" without the symbolism that comes with marriage. It was also defined as recognising "pre-existing" relationships and not those legally created by the state through solemnisation. This principle of "pre-existence", invented to draw a boundary around marriage, flowed on to other areas of LGBTI human rights, including parenting. The consensus in both major parties was that it is acceptable to legally-recognise a same-sex couple who are already parents, but not to change the law to allow them to become parents. This arbitrary distinction, deriving directly from the 2004 same-sex marriage ban, continues to percolate through debates on issues like same-sex adoption.

In 2006 the determination to distinguish between same-sex relationships and marriage manifested itself in another way few people expected. A civil union scheme for same and opposite-sex couples enacted by the ACT Legislative Assembly was refused royal assent by the Governor-General on the advice of John Howard. Before it was quashed, the new law was modified 172 times by the ACT Government to allay Federal Government concern that it was too much like marriage and would somehow fall foul of the 2004 federal marriage amendments, but to no avail. The real and unresolved dispute between the governments at either end of Commonwealth Bridge was that the ACT law solemnised same-sex unions through official ceremonies, in a similar fashion to marriage. In his first term as Prime Minister, Kevin Rudd also opposed ACT Government proposals for a civil union scheme, again on the pretext that this would conflict with the 2004 federal same-sex marriage ban, even though it remained unclear how this conflict actually arose. After its election the Rudd Government invoked the principle of pre-existence by declaring that any ACT scheme could only register existing de facto relationships, not create new legal relationships. Rudd went so far as to misconstrue the Tasmanian relationship registry as a model for an ACT de facto register, even though the Tasmanian scheme does not register de facto relationships, instead creating new legal relationships, through a ceremonial process if the partners wish (for more see chapter 15). In 2009, after two years of haggling, the ACT was allowed a scheme which included ceremonies. But the Federal Government still refused to allow same-sex couples in Canberra to have their relationships solemnised in a way which bore any resemblance to marriage, and still cited the 2004 amendments to justify its meddling in the affairs of a supposedly self-governing territory.

As I've discussed in chapters 1 and 12, the 2004 ban was also used as a pretext to discriminate against Australian same-sex couples seeking to marry overseas. When Australians enter marriages in some overseas jurisdictions they are often required by the government solemnising their union to provide a document called a Certificate of Non-impediment to Marriage (CNI) proving they are not already married in Australia. But when, in August 2005, Vienna-based Australian expatriot, Peter Kakuscka, asked his local Australian consulate for a CNI to marry his male partner in the Netherlands he was refused on the basis that "Australian law does not allow the issue of a Certificate of No Impediment to Marriage to persons wishing to enter into a same-sex marriage". According to then Attorney-

General, Philip Ruddock, this was because the purpose of CNIs is "to certify a proposed marriage would be valid in Australia", a position that was maintained under his Labor successor, Robert McClelland.

Ruddock and McClelland's views were incorrect. As ANU senior law lecturer, Wayne Morgan, has noted,

"There is nothing in Australian law ... that would prevent a Certificate of No Impediment to Marriage (being issued) in such circumstances. This is an internationally accepted document that has nothing to do with the validity of the marriage back in the couple's own country."

The fact is many countries issue CNIs to same-sex partners, even if they themselves do not solemnise same-sex marriages, as was the case in Australia before its prohibition on such marriages was explicitly entrenched. What changed was a new discriminatory definition of marriage which gave Capitol Hill the excuse it needed to reach around the world in an effort to stop LGBTI Australians marrying.

Beyond this preoccupation with delimiting same-sex unions lay an equally strong Government concern about traditionalising heterosexual ones. Another amendment to the Marriage Act, which went largely unnoticed because it was made at the same time as the same-sex marriage ban, defined marriage as the voluntary union for life of one man and one woman to the exclusion of all others. Like the same-sex marriage ban, this amendment was justified by the Howard Government as entrenching in legislation a long-held cultural and common-law assumption about marriage. But as the former Chief Justice of the Family

Court, Alastair Nicholson, has noted, the monogamy-for-life definition of matrimony was outdated even when it was first formulated by Lord Penzance in 1866[186]. It is simply absurd in a nation that allows no-fault divorce. In Nicholson's words,

"What the Government, with the help of the Opposition, has succeeded in doing is to turn back the clock nearly 140 years."

Just as the legislative principle of not allowing same-sex marriages seeped from statute to policy, so did the principle of "turning back the clock" on heterosexual marriages. In the wake of the 2004 amendments, marriage celebrants were bombarded with circulars from the government office which governs their conduct. On top of stern instructions not to conduct unofficial same-sex commitment ceremonies, and not to bow to pressure from marrying couples to drop the ceremonial reference to marriage being "between a man and a woman" in deference to LGBTI wedding guests, the Government insisted that a marrying heterosexual could no longer be referred to by a marriage celebrant as a "partner" or a "person", even if that was the partner's wish. Only the words "husband" and "wife" were admissible in a legally valid ceremony, and only in that order (ironically, at the same time as this policy was announced the decades-old exemption which allowed ministers of religion to vary a marriage ceremony's legal word formula, was also removed). Under the first Rudd Government and much of the Gillard Government nothing changed, despite lobbying from celebrants and community groups. As with the discriminatory policies already cited, there is nothing in the Marriage Act which mandated or required, let alone insisted, on these new policies and regulations. But the 2004 amendments were repeatedly cited to justify them.

'Complementarity is at the root of marriage'

Since 2011 many of these petty regulations have been wound back (for more on this see chapter 2). In December that year the Labor Party's national conference adopted a policy in favour of marriage equality (with a conscience vote for Labor members), and overturned the refusal to give same-sex partners CNIs. Meanwhile, Tasmania and the ACT went on to offer official civil union ceremonies. Celebrants sometimes still receive warnings about not performing non-legal same-sex marriages, although the Government now largely overlooks same-sex commitment ceremonies that don't follow the proscribed marriage ceremony. But the history of the edifice of discrimination built around the 2004 amendments remains important. It is in all the small but telling details of law and policy that we find clues to the broader social vision behind Australia's ban on same-sex marriages.

An obvious part of this vision is entrenching the inferiority of LGBTI people. As I explained in chapter 1, denying us freedom to marry sends the message we are not capable of the level of love and commitment traditionally associated with marriage, and that discrimination on the grounds of sexual orientation is acceptable. To see these attitudes at work one only has to read the repeated declarations by opponents of same-sex marriage that same-sex relationships are too short and unstable to be considered marriages, and that to allow same-sex marriage would "degrade" the institution as a whole. To understand the intensity of hatred behind these declarations one only had to be in the Great Hall of Parliament House on August 13th 2004.

Denying same-sex attracted people freedom to marry marginalises as well as demeans us. Marriage remains a central and highly honoured institution for many Australians. Marriage still provides us the only universally-understood language for love and commitment. It is one of our few institutions which creates kinship. Pointed exclusion from such a valued and universal institution of connection and inclusion sends out the message that LGBTI people cannot fully belong in their families and in society. It says we are the two-dimensional stereotypes so often portrayed.

But more prominent than homophobia, in both the rationale for the same-sex marriage ban and the policy it has been used to justify, is sexual dualism. By this I mean the notion that men and women are intrinsically different and complementary, by virtue of their biological sex, in feeling, intellect and even morality (for more on this see chapter 6). This is the ideology that underlies both Catholic and Evangelical opposition to marriage equality. Pope Francis has declared "the complementarity of man and woman is at the root of marriage and family"[187], as has the Australian Christian Lobby. At the latter's national conference in 2014 an American speaker, Roger Kiska, explained the complementarity of men and women requires them to be "fastened" in marriage"[188].

I assume advocates against same-sex marriages appeal to sexual dualism because it appears less offensive than prejudice against LGBTI people. Certainly, in public discourse they are rarely called upon to explain or justify their view that men and women are complementary in a way which demands they be "fastened". But it is obviously a sexist argument. It assumes that biological sex is a more important feature of an individual than his or her character, abilities or morality. Like almost all generalisations about the difference between men and women, it opens the door to the superiority and dominance of men over women, or at least the precedence of a "husband" over his "wife". The Marriage Act is now the most prominent and influential Australian national law which discriminates on the grounds of sex, as well as sexual orientation. It has become a vehicle for re-introducing a kind of neo-patriarchy.

The third element in the broader social vision underlying the ban on same-sex marriage brings together those I have already mentioned. It is the re-imposition of traditional biblical doctrine through civil law.

To clarify, I am not talking here about the view that marriage is a religious rite or duty, as well as a civil institution. I'm referring to the kind of theocratic outlook that seeks to impose a single set of conservative religious principles on the rest of society – religious and non-religious - by re-making civil marriage according to those principles. Just as there were prison and mission priests who sought to solemnise proscribed marriages for religious reasons, and religious-minded convicts and Aborigines who sought to enter prohibited marriages for the same reasons, so there are many contemporary Australian faith leaders who seek to solemnise same-sex marriages in response to their religious conscience. The imposition of a single set of highly conservative Biblical values on marriage law is as onerous for them as it is for non-religious Australians - so onerous in fact that some of the religious folk who support same-sex marriages have followed in the footsteps of their predecessors by becoming champions of Australia's latest freedom to marry movement.

As I have noted, when the ban on same-sex marriage was first enacted, it was to weld socially-conservative Christian voters to the Howard Government, especially in those key marginal electorates where mega-churches claim significant cultural and economic, as well as spiritual, influence. The first Rudd Government maintained Howard's law, and the policies that accumulated around it, to help it shake some of these voters from the Liberal Party's electoral tree. But when we look more closely at the detail of this ban and what flowed from it, we see that it is not just about appealing to religious prejudices. It is also about entrenching them in law.

To see this we have to look beyond the secular veneer used to disguise the religious motives of some advocates against the freedom of LGBTI people to marry. The Bible is rarely, if ever, quoted to justify denying same-sex partners the freedom to marry. Sometimes religious advocates against reform even disavow the place of religion in their argument, I assume because they feel that in this ever-more-sinful world, God no longer carries the authority He once did. In his evidence to a Senate inquiry into allowing same-sex marriages, Catholic Bishop Peter Elliott opened by declaring,

"...our presentation is not theological. We do not come here to present some Catholic agenda. One of the great traditions

within our faith includes respect for natural law, natural society, the nature of the human person and the good of society....we are here today: not to promote our religion or theology but to promote the natural institution of marriage and family...." [189]

Baptist theologian, Bill Muehlenberg, goes even further. In the book on same-sex marriage we co-authored, Muehlenberg seems to consider it a virtue that religion is absent from his pseudo-scientific case against freedom to marry and chastises me for "playing the religion card" by referring to those Christian denominations that allow same-sex marriages as a part of their religious practice [190].

But despite the overt retreat by opponents of reform from faith as a source of authority, it is still possible to see traditional biblical notions at work in government law and policy-making. Indeed, almost all the important aspects of the same-sex marriage ban I have outlined have a corresponding Biblical base. For many socially-conservative Christians marriage remains primarily a holy rite and same-sex relationships profoundly sinful. Vowing life-long commitment is a sacred command from Jesus, and the duality of the sexes a universal, "natural" principle as old as the Garden of Eden. The Bible even makes sense of the strange, obscure and shaky legal distinction, mentioned above, between laws that create new legal relationships (like marriage) and those that simply recognise existing legal relationships (like de facto marriages and, supposedly, relationship registers). The principle of giving legal recognition to same-sex relationships only if they legally pre-exist reflects the Biblical view that we must have compassion for the fallen while not encouraging or permitting the fall. It is the latest incarnation of the old maxim, love the sinner, hate the sin.

Denying same-sex partners freedom to marry has been the fence-hole through which conservative religious precepts have crept back into Australian law, after they were gradually and rightly removed in the name of equity in the second half of the Twentieth Century. God may not appear, at first glance, to be directing the attempt to reverse these gains. But sherds of Him can still to be found strewn across statutes, and keeping faith with Him is still the raison d'etre of those who do His bidding. The same-sex marriage ban is for law what Intelligent Design is for biology – a way for a traditional, interventionist God to get His foot in secular society's door.

Marriage for its own sake

Allowing same-sex couples to marry will be one of the most effective challenges to the various bigoted beliefs and theocratic fantasies lent legitimacy by the current ban on such marriages. It will ensure we're finally rid of the pile of discriminatory laws and regulations built on the foundation of that ban. But it also has the potential to do much more. First, let's consider what freedom to marry offers same-sex couples, beyond simply legal equity.

Just as early Aboriginal rights advocates, many of them linked to the Labor Party, focused their attention on wages and conditions and overlooked freedom to marry, so some LGBTI rights advocates, again those with links to the ALP, have declared the financial and workplace entitlements of same-sex partners to be a higher priority than the "symbolism" of allowing same-sex marriages. Even among marriage equality advocates there is still a tendency to highlight the practical benefits of the reform, including the legal security and social recognition marriage provide. But when same-sex marriage is seen in the broader context of the freedom to marry its deeper implications are revealed, not least the challenge this freedom issues to one of the most dehumanising stereotypes burdening same-sex attracted people.

In the eyes of those who would deny freedom to marry to any group of people this denial has often been justified by infantilising those from whom the freedom was taken. Convicts were thought to be so lacking in self-control, women so deficient in reason and Aborigines so free of both, that they were incapable of making any important decisions, let alone the decision that is one of the most important any of us is ever called on to make – the choice of a life-long partner. In each case, instead of being allowed to govern their own lives these people had important decisions made for them, for their own good as well as society's. The more important the decision, the more tightly it was regulated, with choice of marriage partner at the top. In equal measure, the granting to these people of the freedom to marry sent out the most powerful message possible that they are capable of morally responsible decisions, and by virtue of this, are fully adult, fully citizens and fully human. The myths often used to justify the denial of freedom to marry to same-sex partners reflect the same kind of infantilisation. Opponents of same-sex marriage carefully deploy images and mis-cite studies to reinforce the myth that LGBTI people are perpetual adolescents – irresponsible, self-centred, frivolous, hormone-driven, out to prove a point, and generally incapable of the reason, self-control, wisdom and foresight needed to make an important life decision and stick to it. As I explain in chapter 1, there are other stereotypes freedom to marry will challenge too, not least that same-sex-attracted people are perpetual outsiders, a threat to children, and less capable of love and commitment. But few stereotypes so completely rob us of our capacity to be considered complete human beings than one that says we do not possess full individual moral responsibility. Allowing LGBTI people freedom to marry will do more than any other single measure to challenge this pervasive stereotype and recognise our equal humanity.

Just as freedom to marry frees LGBTI people to be fully human, so it also frees marriage to be fully marriage. As we have seen, those Australian authorities who have sought to control who ordinary people marry have done so without regard to the values most commonly associated with marriage. Rarely, if ever, have the love a couple share, the welfare of their children, or their desire for the legal, economic, social and/or religious legitimacy and security marriage promises, been sufficient reason for allowing them permission to wed. Instead, marriage for these reasons – we might say marriage for its own sake - is seen as a threat to the broader vision of society held by those who control marriage choice. The threat is so great that unions lying outside the grand plan are demonised as a danger to society. Allowing marriage between people of the wrong racial mix was once seen as threatening Australia's racial integrity, with their children posing such an alarming threat of degeneration they had to be taken away from their parents. Today, opponents of same-sex marriages argue in similar terms that society is somehow threatened by such marriages, and denounce the "moral terrorists" who seek to enter them. In particular they focus on the children raised within such unions, claiming against all the evidence that such children will suffer great harm, and declaring, without a hint of irony, that these children will be the next "Stolen Generation".

But in reality, one of the greatest injuries inflicted by those authorities who turn marriage into a vehicle of ideology is upon marriage itself. When government dictates who can or can't marry, for reasons that have nothing to do with romantic love, raising children, finding personal security, answering religious conscience or anything else traditionally associated with marriage, the credibility and appeal of the institution is impaired. When the justification for this intervention demonises those who seek to marry, again because they are in love and/or want to raise children, the link between marriage and its conventional meanings is broken.

For those who value marriage, the obvious question is, can this damage be undone? In Australia, governmental interference with the freedom to marry in the name of a broader social vision has occurred so often, and with so little regard to the meaning or values of marriage, it is tempting to think it is a pattern the nation cannot escape. An argument can be made that when the state responded to the chaos and dislocation of early colonial life, and took advantage of the abject legal status of a majority of its citizens, by assuming control over arranging their marriages, it fell into a bureaucratic habit that it cannot shake, inscribing the manipulation of marriage into the nation's political and cultural DNA forever. But a society is more than the state that governs it. Australians have the choice to break the bad habits of successive governments. Right now, the most important step we can take in this direction is to allow same-sex partners our freedom to marry. Allowing LGBTI Australians to rule our own lives may not redeem marriage and the nation from all the flawed and failed attempts to reconfigure the latter by manipulating the former. But it may just stop it happening again.

15. Flight from the gilded cage: addressing criticism of marriage equality from the left

"Traditional marriage is a rotten oppressive institution.... Marriage is a contract which smothers both people, denies needs, and places impossible demands on both people...Gay people must stop gauging their self respect by how well they mimic straight marriages. To accept that happiness comes through finding a groovy spouse and settling down, showing the world that 'we're just the same as you" is avoiding the real issues, and is an expression of self-hatred.

Refugees from Amerika: A Gay Manifesto
Carl Wittman, 1970

At various points in this book I have addressed the case against marriage equality made by social and religious conservatives. I have also advanced the reasons conservatives should support the reform: it promotes healthy, stable and committed relationships, protects children, fosters financial self-reliance, enhances religious freedom, and ultimately preserves the institution of marriage.

But there are also objections from the left; from people who lay claim to some form of feminism, gay liberation, post modernism, sexual radicalism, socialism, social criticism, unconventionality or outsider status to justify their antagonism to marriage equality. Their arguments may originate in a wide array of ideologies and world views, but they almost all converge at the same point

– admiration for the sexual creativity and license they associate with same-sex relationships and a loathing of the restrictions and dull conformity they believe marriage brings. Some grant the principle of legal equality, but almost all remain baffled and even affronted by same-sex couples marrying and the campaign to allow it.

Criticism of marriage equality from the left is too often ignored by proponents of reform. Such objections are more likely to be an irritant in a university seminar room than a hurdle in an MP's office. But objections from the left have the potential over time to sap the enthusiasm political progressives have for marriage equality. They also provide ammunition for conservative opponents of change, especially if the marriage equality critic being quoted is gay.

Right wing marriage equality opponents like Baptist theologian, Bill Muehlenberg, are adept at deploying gay opponents of marriage equality in their advocacy. Muehlenberg frequently quotes gay men and lesbians who criticise marriage, poke fun at it, want to abolish or escape it, question the need for equality within it, or just don't want to get married. But these are the diverse responses you would expect in any group of people to an institution as universal as marriage. A far larger number of heterosexuals have been criticising, satirising and avoiding matrimony for centuries. If this were a legitimate basis to exclude whole groups from marriage, no-one would be allowed to marry.

The reason people like Muehlenberg cite gay opponents of marriage equality is not just because they want to create the misleading impression that the LGBTI community is hopelessly divided on the reform (surveys consistently show over 80% of LGBTI people support it). There is a surprising similarity between the arguments used by opponents of marriage equality on the right and the left that is immensely useful for the former and should be more than a little embarrassing to the latter. The most striking similarity is the way both groups mischaracterise marriage and same-sex relationships in order to make the two seem irreconcilable.

On the marriage tram

Like opponents of marriage equality on the right, critics on the left portray marriage as a conservative and conservatising institution that is religious, male-dominated and sexually restrictive. In the left's white-picket-fence version of marriage, women are subordinated, sex is always in the missionary position, couples are generally unhappy and hypocrisy thrives. The only real winner is rigid social order.

According to Fairfax columnist, Clementine Ford,

"...marriage remains a largely conservative institution founded on the monocultural ideals of a two-parent nuclear family". (For many people marriage is) "a patriarchal tradition rooted in the belief that women were a form of economic and property trade". [191]

Coming even more directly to the point, US marriage equality critics, Dan Spade and Craig Willse, declare

"...all forms of marriage perpetuate gender, racial and economic inequality." [192]

Australian commentator, Jessica Kean, sees this view of marriage as the reason Julia Gillard opposed marriage equality when she was Prime Minister.

"She (Gillard) did not balk at the thought of recognising same-sex relationships as valuable, but rather at the thought that we would, as a secular and progressive Australia, put all our eggs in the basket of a tradition steeped in sexual moralism and gendered inequality. As a woman and feminist in a long term non-marriage partnership she has taken a strong public stance against the idea that the legitimacy of a union rests on the ability to put a ring on it." [193]

While this assessment of Julia Gillard's motives may be correct, it misses the point that a core principle of feminism is choice. As a partner in a different-sex relationship, Gillard had a choice to marry. She betrayed her principles by denying that choice to others.

Critics on the left despise their conservative image of marriage as much as opponents from the right idealise theirs. But both groups make two key mistakes. The first is that they generalise wildly, like Spade and Willse, ignoring the diverse ways in which heterosexual couples have conducted their marriages across different cultures and eras. The second mistake is that they see marriage as it once was, not what it has become. As I noted in chapter 5 , marriage today is not the compulsory, one-size-fits-all, church-backed cultural monolith it was fifty years ago. Thanks to greater social acceptance of de facto relationships, civil marriage, contraception, divorce and women's equality, partners are now freer to choose for themselves if, when and why they marry, how to conduct their marriage and if and when to end it. Reflecting on her opposition to marriage equality during a meeting with advocates in 2012, Julia Gillard described a metaphorical tram heading away from marriage that she and her fellow Melbourne University graduates had alighted in the 1960s. She noted that the tram was now almost empty and most of the other former students had gotten on the marriage tram[194]. This is because the marriage tram kept up with them.

The forebears of today's feminists and liberationists fought hard and successfully to modernise marriage, in particular to remove the absolute control of the church, and to ensure husbands and wives are equal. Without the transformation of attitudes and laws these reformers initiated there would be no campaign for same-sex marriage. The idea would be inconceivable. Critics of marriage equality on the left should see the reform as a vindication of this generations-long battle to bring greater equity, choice and humanity to sexual and family life, not a retreat from it. They should see marriage equality as removing one of the final examples of explicit sexism from the law and drawing a clearer line between the secular and religious spheres. They should grasp that a site of discrimination can also be, indeed is likely to be, a site of freedom. The history of the struggle for interracial marriage in Australia and the US is a perfect example (see chapter 14 for more). Some of today's right wing opponents of marriage equality are using the Marriage Act and the movement against reforming it to foster neo-patriarchal and neo-theocratic values: their talk of the "complementary roles" of men and women can be code for male dominance, while their rhetoric about protecting religious freedom too often means enforcing religious values using the law (for more see chapter 14). Supporting marriage equality is the most direct way to counter these insidious trends.

Even if some feminists don't grasp this, there are plenty who do. In chapter 12 I mentioned Lee and Sandra who wish to marry before Lee dies. Lee had been a Labor voter for almost half a century and was involved in a wide range of social causes, including the rights of indigenous people, anti-Vietnam War protests and support groups for lesbian women in rural areas. In April 2015, when I was invited to a dinner with Julia Gillard, I asked Lee what message she would like me to pass on. This is what she wrote:

"I would like you to know that you have been a guiding light for the equality for women and you have had my full support and admiration. I have been a staunch Labor supporter since 1966 and strongly fought for feminist issues and equality for all. Please help switch on the light for same-sex marriage and take us out of the darkness."

Outlaws or in-laws?

As well as portraying marriage as more conservative than it really is, opponents of marriage equality on both the left and right portray same-sex relationships as more radical than they actually are. Some left wing critics of marriage equality maintain that same-sex couples are more emotionally creative and sexually open than their heterosexual counterparts. According to MJ Kaufman and Katie Miles.

"...we strongly believe that queers are not like everyone else. Queers are sexy, resourceful, creative, and brave enough to challenge an oppressive system with their lifestyle." [195]

This flattering stereotype is easy for some LGBTI people to accept because it dignifies their status as outsiders and gives them a liberating mission. It is easy for some heterosexuals to accept because it allows them to project titillating fantasies on to homosexuals. But it is no less offensive than its more common derogatory counterparts. It marginalises LGBTI people who are not "sexy, resourceful, creative, and brave" just the same way sex radicals say they feel marginalised by marriage equality. Worse, it leads directly to the chauvinistic stance that same-sex relationships are fundamentally and irreconcilably different to different-sex relationships. Some left wing opponents of marriage equality use words like "mimicry" and "homo-normativity" to shame those same-sex couples who want to marry for ignoring their difference and "pretending" to be like heterosexuals. It's telling that the religious right uses the word "mimicry" in exactly the same way.

Let's have a closer look at the imagined difference between gay and straight that is said to put the former at odds with marriage. Whence does this difference derive and how does it manifest itself? Like conservative opponents of marriage equality, gay academic and marriage sceptic, Dennis Altman, believes gay monogamy is a myth, although he thinks this is a good thing.

"It does seem clear that among gay men a long-lasting monogamous relationship is almost unknown. Indeed

both gay women and gay men tend to be involved in what might be called multiple relationships, though of somewhat different kinds.[196] *"...We don't find one partner sufficiently fulfilling."* [197]

And like his conservative counterparts, Altman justifies this with studies that are not representative.

"A large-scale study of gay male couples in San Diego concluded that every couple together more than five years had outside sexual contacts as a recognised part of the relationship." [198]

The 1983 study Altman relies on, by David McWhirter and Andrew Mattison, only involved 156 couples drawn mostly from gay friendship networks in one inner city gay ghetto[199]. The study was pioneering in its day but doesn't stack up against today's far larger studies, with samples in the thousands, that show same-sex and different-sex relationships to be very much the same in terms of domestic and sexual arrangements. I cite some of these studies in chapter 5.

For the lesbian law theorist and marriage equality opponent, Paula Ettelbrick, the difference between same-sex and different-sex relationships is chiefly political not sociological.

"As a lesbian, I am fundamentally different from non-lesbian women....Being queer is more than setting up house, sleeping with a person of the same gender, and seeking state approval for doing so. ... Being queer means pushing the parameters of sex, sexuality, and family, and in the process, transforming the very fabric of society." [200]

Ettelbrick runs up against the same problem facing Kaufman and Miles. What about those lesbians who do not wish to fundamentally transform society or do not see their relationship as transforming anything but their own lives? Are they lesser lesbians? Is their aspiration to be included in a long-standing social institution to be sacrificed to the revolutionary dreams of others? If so, Ettelbrick is perpetrating a kind of tyranny by using the law to impose her values. If not, she has perpetuated a stereotype as harmful as any.

Gay author and broadcaster, Robert Dessaix, turns to literature rather than social science or the law to make his case that homosexuals are, or should be, too different to heterosexuals to be part of an institution like marriage and all he thinks it represents.

"The one marvellous thing about being homosexual in the West over the past few decades is that you have been free to love and be loved - for a season, forever, deeply, sexually, asexually, emotionally, faithfully, promiscuously, wildly, gently, in a couple, a threesome, a foursome, however it suits you - without getting married. For a time, homosexuals were proud of being different. They once wrote novels and plays about being different. They lived the lives of sexual aristocrats, not pillars of suburbia, grabbing life by the throat with a shout and a flourish before it strangled them for being as different as they were. Now the streets are swarming with men and women who demand the right to be common. They can't wait to be monogamously married, with children, to be husbands and wives, just like all the other couples in the street. Why this rush back to a middle-American fantasy from the 1950s? Do they imagine it will at last give them the right to hold hands in Target?" [201]

I've already addressed the caricature of marriage Dessaix, like too many others, lazily draws on. Just as the world has changed since the 1950s, so has marriage. The particular mistake he makes is to assume homosexuals were once all one thing and are now all its opposite. In fact, there has always been a small minority of sexual radicals and a much, much larger group of homosexuals who are anything but. As tolerance of homosexuality has increased the latter group has found its voice and that voice demands simply the freedom to live their lives untainted by prejudice and discrimination. You can call it the freedom to hold hands in Target, and in part it is, but it something much greater. It is the freedom of every LGBTI person to live their life as they choose. It is the democratisation of gay identity. Dessaix's elitist alternative, the "freedom" to be a sexual aristocrat, is simply the cold hard fact of exclusion magically transformed into a comforting conceit. He would have us all live in a gilded cage, and one where the gilding is wearing off. As Pulitzer Prize winning author, Philip Kennicott, found when he revisited the canon of gay sexual rebels like Gide, Genet, Cocteau, Wilde, Baldwin and Mann, what once seemed revolutionary is now just "sad, furtive and destructive"[202].

In the eyes of one of the world's greatest living gay writers, Edmund White, it's far more liberating to take flight from the gilded cage than live in it:

"In the past, when gays were very flamboyant as drag queens or as leather queens or whatever, that just amused people. And most of the people that come and watch the gay Halloween parade, where all those excesses are on display, those are straight families, and they think it's funny. But what people don't think is so funny is when two middle-aged lawyers who are married to each other move in next door to you and your

wife and they have adopted a Korean girl and they want to send her to school with your children and they want to socialize with you and share a drink over the backyard fence. That creeps people out, especially Christians. So, I don't think gay marriage is a conservative issue. I think it's a radical issue." [203]

Like Dessaix, White makes the mistake of assuming LGBTI people were once more radical than we really were. It is not we who have changed but the world's view of us. I'm also uneasy with the implication that gay suburbanisation can be seen as a political strategy when it is actually the product of complex and largely unconscious social changes. But White is right that moving beyond traditional and very limiting stereotypes is the most important thing LGBTI people and the broader community can do.

Just as marriage equality seals rather than undermines generations of reform promoting gender equity and secularism in marriage law, so it is the fulfilment, not the repudiation, of the struggle of generations of LGBTI freedom fighters. Altman, Ettlebrick and Dessaix might not value the freedom to marry and form a conventional family, but this aspiration sprang inevitably from the calls of early gay advocates for personal self-determination, for freedom from the prejudices of others, and an end to stigma and shame. They may think the choice to marry is a flawed one but it was always the goal of the gay movement to allow gay people to "be judged by the content of their character" not their sexual orientation or gender identity. They may want homosexuals to be outlaws, not in-laws. But both aspirations arose from the same demand for respect and freedom.

"Self-indulgent crap"

The parallels between the right wing and left wing cases against marriage equality don't end at similar misconceptions about what marriage has become and who homosexuals are. Both groups try to delegitimise the demand for marriage equality by pretending it is contrived and political. The anti-equality right says it's only an issue because the Greens keep pushing it, or because of some left wing conspiracy to undermine traditional values. The anti-marriage left says it is only an issue because a decade ago conservatives like John Howard and George W Bush used it to wedge the left and corral conservative voters. Left wing commentator, Guy Rundle, goes even further. In a re-invention of the old-left view that marriage is an instrument of capitalism, a way to create a more orderly and productive workforce, Rundle lays the blame for marriage equality at the feet of the individualised, contract-based culture created by free market ideology.

"...the path to marriage equality didn't begin five years ago – it began, you might say, when Sunday trading was abolished and capital finally triumphed over the Sabbath, quashing any notion that the state should have any regard to traditional values in setting the rules. It's only after a period in which capital has made all cultural barriers to individual wants into a denial of human rights that the campaign became possible – because marriage equality cuts with the cultural grain of neoliberalism." [204]

Rundle, like critics of marriage equality on the right, ignores the long history of marriage equality going back decades, the deep, generations-long demographic and cultural changes driving it, and the links between freedom to marry for mixed-race and same-sex couples (see chapter 11 and chapter 1, respectively). This makes it easier for him to abuse the ideal of liberty by equating the real freedom of two loving partners to marry with the "freedom" of a supermarket chain to open all the time and crush corner stores.

Critics on the left also have their own version of the right's line that marriage equality is a low priority and a distraction from economic issues (see chapter 9). They argue there are more important LGBTI and/or left wing issues from which resources and focus are being diverted. Some believe marriage equality robs transgender and intersex issues of the attention they deserve, others that challenging homophobia in schools or preventing LGBTI youth suicide is a higher priority, and others, still, that LGBTI persecution overseas is being sidelined. Dennis Altman thinks marriage equality is

"…a great deal of self-indulgent crap. I mean people around the world are being tortured for being homosexual and people here carry on as if not being allowed to marry was a huge abuse of civil rights." [205]

Leading left author, John Pilger, goes further, suggesting that Barack Obama's evolution on marriage equality was designed to distract attention from America's wars and from economic inequality.

"When Obama recently announced he supported same-sex marriage, American planes had not long blown 14 Afghan civilians to bits…the mass murder was barely news. What mattered were the cynical vacuities of a political celebrity, the

product of a zeitgeist driven by the forces of consumerism and the media with the aim of diverting the struggle for social and economic justice." [206]

The lack of consensus on which issues marriage equality distracts us from suggests the real problem for left wing critics, as it is among those on the right, is that they just don't like marriage equality being talked about. But let's assume for the sake of argument that the criticism is sincerely put. One obvious response is that the marriage equality debate actually brings many of these other issues to the fore. Never have LGBTI issues been more discussed in Australia's parliaments than they are today either because they come up within the context of marriage equality, or because dealing with them gives politicians an excuse not to deal with marriage equality. Excellent examples of this are the new-found enthusiasm of federal politicians who oppose marriage equality to vote for transgender anti-discrimination protections and funding for school anti-homophobia programs, and of their counterparts at a state level to support the expungement of gay criminal records and same-sex adoption. Regardless, in my experience LGBTI advocates are skilled enough to make more than one case at once and the broader Australian community is sophisticated enough to hear them.

The criticism concerning the situation overseas is even more misguided. Anti-gay legislators in Russia, Africa and Asia believe they are fighting a global tide of immorality and would feel vindicated by Australia failing to achieve marriage equality. In a recent overview of world homophobia, American writer, Jeff Sharlet, lists Australia along with Russia, central Africa and India as places where "anti-gay crusaders are developing new laws and sharpening old ones". Sharlet sees what too many Australians can't: the campaign to keep marriage inequality in Australia has become one of the far right's key battlegrounds in its war on modernity[207]. Australian columnist, Tim Dick, is a welcome exception to the Australian left's failure to draw these links. He believes marriage equality is the first thing Australia can do to help "our persecuted kin" in the developing world.

"The further it spreads, the greater the proof that civilisation does not collapse when the law accepts different kinds of love. When the example spreads to emerging economies, it can't be written off as the depravity of the West. Hello, Uruguay! But the West needs to be solid in support. So Canberra, for our sake and that of the rest of humanity, get on with it." [208]

Equally, advocates across the world, from New Zealand to the UK, Ireland and the US, have been inspired by the creativity and persistence of the Australian marriage equality campaign. Many would be demoralised by its failure. Campaigning for marriage equality in Australia, far from being a distraction from the plight of LGBTI people in other countries, is a duty we owe to them.

As for Pilger, his case diminishes both the importance of legal equality for minorities and the capacity of the public to see with a clear eye the good and the bad in a particular administration. He may as well be arguing that presidents Kennedy and Johnson supported the black civil rights movement to distract attention from the Vietnam War. All forms of entrenched inequality – economic, social, legal, racial, religious and sexual – are demeaning and demand action to overturn them. To privilege, say, economic inequality over legal inequality, as Pilger does, is to risk marginalising same-sex couples in just the same way other critics of marriage equality claim it marginalises transgender folk. The dystopic elements of too many socialist societies have their roots in this kind of reductionism.

Remember Stonewall!

A counterpart to the claim that marriage equality is a confected issue or one that arose on the right, is the claim that it is a betrayal of the true origins of the LGBTI movement. This contribution to *Against Equality*, a book of left-wing essays against marriage equality, is a good example of the claim:

"The origins of the LGBTIQ movement are revolutionary. The rebellions at Stonewall and San Francisco City Hall were led by drag queens and butches who rejected heterosexual roles and restrictions, who were inspired by the revolutionary example of the Black panthers and the Womens International Terrorist Conspiracy from Hell (WITCH)." [209]

Again, we can see a parallel with some right wing opponents of marriage equality, specifically those who claim that allowing same-sex couples to marry is a betrayal of the religious origins of marriage. In both cases, good polemic makes for very bad history. LGBTI movements in different nations go back decades before police raids on the Stonewall Inn in the summer of 1969 prompted the bar's gay and transgender patrons to pelt the police and torch cars. These other movements had vastly different origins and trajectories to the one suggested above. For example, in Nineteenth Century Berlin, the first place with an LGBTI rights movement, German idealism and romanticism played a key role in shaping gay activists' outlook and aspirations[210]. Secularism, anti-clericalism and Catholic conceptions of social justice and liberation have significantly influenced movements in Southern Europe and Latin America. In Eastern Europe the contemporary LGBTI movement sprang from the movement against Communism in the late 1980s. At about the same time in my homeland of Tasmania the environment movement gave rise to the LGBTI rights movement. In the US itself, gay rights advocacy, back to the 1940s and earlier, was heavily influenced by the black civil rights movement and reverted quickly to its roots when the revolutionary impulses of those who initially mythologised Stonewall as a new departure faded after a few years.

LGBTI rights movements are far older, more diverse and more open to marriage equality than opponents of the reform are willing to concede. The elevation of one, exceptional moment in US LGBTI history to the status of a pivot upon which all LGBTI history swung devalues this diversity. It also devalues this event itself by limiting it meaning. Participants in the Stonewall Riot, and the political events that flowed in its wake, had a variety of different motivations and goals. Some turned Stonewall into an impetus for community building and for homosexual law reform. Some were just jack of police heavy-handedness. To today's reformers, Stonewall stands as a warning of the repression and desperation that can come from abandoning our efforts, as much as it stands in the eyes of revolutionaries for the flames that alone can purify the world.

"Risky consequences"

Opponents of marriage equality on the left and the right have symmetrical narratives about what, in their view, are the dubious origins of the marriage equality campaign and the damage they believe that campaign is doing now. Not surprisingly there is also a symmetry when it comes to the "unintended consequences" of the reform. I have already mentioned some of the fears of the right about the violation of religious freedoms and a slippery slope to polygamy and bestiality. On the left the fear is that marriage equality will create a hierarchy between "respectable" married same-sex couples, and "less legitimate" unmarried couples, singles and sexual outsiders. In another echo of the right, some left critics even claim couples who don't want to marry will be coerced to[211]. As I've already noted, there is also a fear LGBTI people will lose their distinctiveness and be assimilated by mainstream culture.

Australian academic, Annamarie Jagose, is concerned that

"In recognising some gay and lesbian relationships as marriages, same-sex marriage emphasises the continued illegitimacy of other sexual arrangements and the continued exclusion of other social actors. The legalisation of same-sex marriage has risky consequences that exceed the good intentions of many of those arguing for it. Therefore, the recognition of same-sex couples through marriage is not a wholly benign or even a neutral act because, like the historic form of marriage itself, it recognises the worth of some relationships by valuing them more than others." [212]

Who does she fear is being left out in the cold?

"...those whose erotic lives are not organised around the values symbolised by marriage: coupledom, monogamy, permanence, domestic cohabitation. Unmarried mothers, for instance; adulterers; the devotedly promiscuous; sex workers; the divorced; single people.... Now this ragtag bunch might not seem as worthy of social protection and prestige as the loving, caring, long-term gay and lesbian couples that are the shiny new poster boys and girls for same-sex marriage. But it reminds us to ask something that advocates of same-sex marriage, in their eagerness, forget to ask: why should marriage continue in the 21st century to be a primary mechanism for the distribution of social recognition and privilege?"

I fail to grasp Jagose's social calculus. Exactly how does including same-sex couples within an institution that should not bar us increase the social exclusion of other people who choose not to marry, are not in a marriage-like relationship or are not even in a relationship? Will sex workers feel more devalued when same-sex couples can marry because there are fewer people to share their outsider status? Jagose's link is as abstract and unreal as the link right wing critics draw between same-sex marriages and heterosexuals feeling their marriages are devalued. Worse still is the cynicism about any reforming project implicit in Jagose's stance. To argue that the inclusion of one group exacerbates the exclusion of another, or that the exclusion of some groups justifies the continued exclusion of all, is to argue against any prospect of social progress.

But there is a more immediate issue posed by Jagose's question about the privileged position of marriage. Are marriage equality advocates ignoring, even reinforcing, a hierarchy of love? In my experience the answer is "no". Many of Australia's long-time advocates for marriage equality are respectful of people who choose not to marry and have worked hard to ensure their relationships have legal protection and recognition, including through the recognition of same-sex de facto and registered relationships. I too have dedicated years of my life to these campaigns. This included the drafting and passage of landmark Tasmanian relationship legislation since adopted in several other Australian states. This legislation gave the legal rights and recognition traditionally reserved for married heterosexuals not just to unmarried heterosexual and same-sex couples but to all other forms of significant personal relationship including older companions, carers and the people they care for, and Indigenous people in traditional kinship bonds. This extension of spousal entitlements to partners because they share their lives, not just a bed, casts the law's net more widely than Jagose's narrow focus on "erotic life".

Under the Tasmanian law no cohabitation is required before a relationship is recognised. Neither is there a requirement for partners to have shared finances, make a life-long commitment, or have a sexual relationship. Similarly, partners decide for themselves whether they want their relationship recognised through a civil partnership with an official ceremony, a civil partnership without a ceremony, or for it simply to be presumed to exist. It is essentially in the hands of ordinary citizens, not the state, to define which of their relationships they want legally recognised, and when and how this recognition should occur. No other scheme for the recognition of relationships anywhere in the world is less hierarchical and more democratic.

At no point was the Tasmanian scheme meant as a substitute for same-sex marriage, or marriage more broadly, like some of the more marriage-like civil union schemes that have been implemented elsewhere. Instead, the Tasmanian scheme was meant as an alternative for couples who can't or don't want to marry. Rather than being developed as a politically-expedient solution to the demand for marriage equality the Tasmanian scheme is based on a set of principles, foremost equity and choice. These two principles are behind my advocacy for both the Tasmanian scheme and for marriage equality so I see no inconsistency between the two. Both expand the possibilities for the recognition of loving relationships.

I firmly believe history is on the side of these principles. Unmarried relationships are increasingly recognised legally and accepted socially. Not an eyebrow was raised by Prince William and Kate Middleton – the future king and queen of England – "living in sin". It's true that in many parts of the United States the only path to spousal entitlements is down the aisle. But with the equal recognition of unmarried cohabiting partners this is no longer the case in Australia and most other parts of the western world. The recognition of non-conjugal relationships, pioneered in Tasmania, is also occurring in other places. Just as the choice not to marry is increasingly respected so is the choice to be single. Of course, many people still see marriage as a gold standard of relationships. But that is less and less the case. Marriage is increasingly seen by heterosexual couples as a choice they are free to make without legal or social prejudice, and a choice same-sex couples should be free to make too.

Don't take my word for it. Look at the evidence, or lack of it. If critics like Jagose are correct, then in places with marriage equality we would expect to see increased levels of prejudice against unmarried partners, unpartnered people or those who don't live in marriage-like relationships. Laws recognising cohabiting partners would be rolled back. Children born out of wedlock would endure increased stigma. Underground inner-city sexual cultures would have been swept away in the rush to the suburbs. Same-sex couples who felt "coerced" into marriage would be grumbling about it. But there is no evidence of any of this. Yes, prejudice persists against those who can't or don't marry, but viewed in the long term it is waning not waxing. Just as marriage equality is not the apocalypse defenders of "traditional values" fear, so it has not sent acceptance of different personal choices into a sudden reverse.

Emancipation and integration

The other big "unintended consequence" of marriage equality feared by its left wing critics is assimilation.

Writing on marriage equality in the Melbourne University student magazine Farrago, Curtis Red emphatically makes the point:

"Have we given up on liberation and settled for assimilation? The old chants of "fuck off breeder scum" have been replaced with "we're just like you"; as we beg for a place at the table of heteronormativity. Instead of critiquing a system and an institution that structurally oppresses us as queers we are lining

up to be good heterogays and disappear into the suburbs with our superannuation, mortgages and tax cuts." [213]

LGBTI people have always lived in the suburbs and wrestled with superannuation and mortgages. The right to marry will recognise in law what is already true in everyday life: most LGBTI people live pretty conventional lives as members of their families and communities. Marriage equality is not a betrayal of their destiny but an affirmation of it. What's more, as I have already discussed in chapter 11, a western-world-wide demographic shift has seen more and more LGBTI people stay in, or move to, suburban and regional areas. In part, the demand for marriage equality arose from this demographic shift, but it did not set it off. Greater legal and social tolerance did that. Evidence lies in the fact the shift has been strong in Australia without marriage equality. I suspect what we are seeing in people like Curtis Red is a failure to face the underlying causes of a trend he doesn't like. Instead, he blames marriage equality because it's an easy target. This mirrors those on the right who decry what they believe is the decline of marriage but feel powerless to tackle the underlying reasons and use same-sex marriage as a scapegoat (for more on this see chapter 5). Whatever Red's motive, his caricature of LGBTI people and our history confuses cause and effect.

A more serious source of confusion from people like Red is their false dichotomy between liberation and assimilation. There is another option, one that has been pursued by every religious and racial minority since the Enlightenment: emancipation and integration. This was the noble goal of European Jews in the Eighteenth and Nineteenth centuries and African Americans and Aboriginal Australians in the Twentieth. It was the vision that drove civil rights heroes like Martin Luther King Jnr and Nelson Mandela. And at the core of each of these movements for emancipation and integration was the demand for members of the minority in question to marry freely (for more on this see chapters 1 and 14).

For the most part, leaders of these various movements did not fear valuable cultural traditions and identities would be lost through integration. They understood there is a critical distinction between providing everyone with equal rights and expecting everyone to be the same. Indeed, many looked forward to the great cultural flowering to come. History vindicated their optimism. For example, when Europe's Jews were released from their ghettos they didn't all suddenly cease to be Jews. They were freer to identify, to whatever degree they chose, with their inherited ethnic and religious identity, and to enrich the broader society of which they had become a part with whatever they considered valuable about this identity. The result was a contribution to western culture from the descendants of emancipated Jews - Mendelssohn, Marx, Kafka, Freud, Wittgenstein and Einstein - that was unthinkable while the ghetto lasted, and without which the contemporary world would be utterly different.

I imagine the same future for LGBTI people. As we are freer to interact with the society around us in more complex ways, so we will also make a far richer contribution to that society than is possible today, a contribution drawn from but not limited by our sexual or gender identities. Integration will not mean we vanish but that we flourish.

It will affirm that we do not have a separate destiny but a shared one. Marriage equality will be an integral part of this process. As I've argued, allowing same-sex couples to marry will not profoundly change marriage or LGBTI people. Culturally and legally each has already grown to meet the other. There is certainly no evidence from countries with marriage equality that same-sex couples have been unwillingly assimilated, just as there is also no evidence minorities previously denied freedom to marry, like African Americans or Aboriginal Australians, lost their cultural traditions and distinctiveness when granted this freedom. Instead, like other steps towards legal equality and social integration, marriage equality will mean LGBTI people are increasingly free to contribute to society all that we are, including the experience we have gained from being excluded, from our struggle to end that exclusion, and from what it means to finally belong.

Abolishing marriage

Given the many parallels between the right and left wing cases against same-sex marriages, it's not surprising that the ultimate solution posed by many in both camps is also strikingly similar. Having mythologised marriage as the repository of everything they hate, but still believing in equity, some on the left resolve that the best response to the demand of same-sex couples for equality is to abolish marriage altogether. It is not always entirely clear what is meant by "abolish". Some mean repealing the Marriage Act so the state is no longer involved in solemnising and entitling lifelong, committed relationships. Instead, some other form of relationship recognition would bestow legal entitlements and the word "marriage" would only apply to religious ceremonies. This is what US academic Tamara Metz means when she writes of "disestablishing" marriage[214]. But there are others for whom the abolition of marriage means wiping away every legal and cultural vestige of the institution. When they speak with such relish and conviction about the inevitable demise of marriage I can't help hearing those utopians who once talked about the withering away of the state or the death of God.

Disestablishing marriage resonates on the libertarian right with people like Australian Freedom Commissioner, Tim Wilson, favouring its "privatisation".

"I have always argued the best thing we could do to deal with the issue - and I don't even like the term marriage equality - is to get the government out of marriage; it's to privatise the contracts, for want of a better phrase. That is what marriage is; it is a contract between two parties - and sometimes, in spirit, a third called God, or some other higher being - a contract between parties. I would rather see - rather than the government saying this is what marriage is and this is how it is defined - to get out of it all together and hand it back to the church and say you have your marriage."

This course of action is also beginning to resonate among religious conservatives. As marriage equality strides across the United States some traditional religious opponents of the reform are proposing that religious celebrants retreat from the solemnisation of legal marriages and only perform legally-irrelevant religious marriage ceremonies. The hard edge of their concern is that the state will, at some point, force them to perform same-sex marriages. But there is a broader context. More and more US and

Australian conservative religious leaders are lamenting the decline in their political influence from a high point of the mid-2000s. They are returning to an older evangelical tradition of spurning political involvement as ungodly. It is hard to see churches relinquishing the legal and cultural clout they have by virtue of being contracted by the government to perform legal marriages, even if this clout, like the number of church weddings, is on the slide. But the desire for purity and separation – the one that saw religious dissidents risk all by relocating to America and Australia in the first place – is growing stronger in some religious circles.

So, is removing the state from marriage a realistic response to the demand for marriage equality? It certainly isn't politically feasible. Despite the theoretical musings of academics and activists, marriage remains a legal and social status to which many people aspire. Indeed, in most western countries the proportion of married couples is increasing. The aspiration to marry remains strong among the young, even if more of them are delaying the day. Wedding vows of mutual fidelity, care and support obviously mean something to the millions of citizens who continue to make and uphold them. The relative increase in civil marriages shows that these vows, and the state-guaranteed legal security that comes with them, still matter even when religion isn't involved. For these reasons, nowhere in the world is a serious demand being made, a movement built, or a bill proposed, to abolish marriage and find a replacement. To respond to the demand for marriage equality by proposing the abolition of marriage, either legally or culturally, is at best naïve or at worst a cynical ploy to avoid addressing the issue.

Even if the abolition of marriage was politically possible, is it desirable? The ubiquity of marriage across different times and cultures, as well as its continued popularity today, hint at the institution's deep roots. Not only do these roots run deep in law and history, they also seem to run deep in our psychology. Clearly, many people, regardless of their age, gender, social origins or political outlook, still value the opportunity to make a legally recognised vow of enduring commitment to one other person. Perhaps this is because of an intuitive understanding of what science is increasingly telling us about the value of enduring relationships. Perhaps it is a reaction against the pressures of a culture of consumerism. Whatever the reason, marriage has shown itself to be far more resilient and less fragile than those on the right fear and those on the left hope.

That marriage seems so entrenched makes me wonder if its legal abolition would have the desired effect of erasing it culturally. The aspiration to make marriage-like vows and live in an enduring relationship could well shape whatever might replace marriage into a new form of what went before. It wouldn't be the first time the persistence of popular expectations defied attempts by ideologues and social engineers to remove them. Given the lack of political or community interest in abolishing marriage, I guess we'll never know.

Why left wing critics of marriage equality should support it

Many of today's left wing critics of lifting the ban on same-sex marriages would have been in the front line of protests against the legal bans on interracial marriage, no-fault divorce and gay sex. Their commitment to equal opportunity and choice would have driven them there. But when it comes to marriage equality their commitment fails them and their values fade away. They have developed various intellectual strategies to quarantine yesterday's struggles from today's. But these are often backward looking, reliant on stereotypes about marriage and LGBTI people, based on unfounded fears, ridden with abstractions or just plain utopian. Tellingly, after a decade of questioning marriage equality they have no new arguments against it. The critics of marriage equality are trapped in an intellectual cul-de-sac.

How can we free them? How can we bring their intellectual and moral weight to bear on marriage equality in a way that will move them and the issue forward? The answer is the same as it is for conservative critics of marriage equality: an appeal to their fundamental values. At various points in this discussion I've referred to some of the politically progressive outcomes of marriage equality. These include challenging those who would write Leviticus into law by separating civil legislation and religious values, challenging those who seek to control the lives of others by providing ordinary people with greater choice about how they live their own lives, and challenging the global, neo-patriarchal movement seeking to marginalise women and punish LGBTI people (for more on some of the ideas driving this movement see chapter 14). This last point may by the most important of all. The 2008 financial crisis gave rise to a global movement against the concentration of wealth and power in the hands of ever fewer people.

This new movement also challenges the attempts by some powerful interests to divide and rule by fostering religious, racial, class and sexual hatreds. The ideal of this movement is greater equity in everything from political power and economic opportunities through health and education to the treatment of minority communities. Marriage equality fits neatly within that ideal.

But if appeals to progressive values fail, there is one final way to win over sceptics of marriage equality (apart from attendance at an actual same-sex wedding which in my experience will soften the hardest heart but is not yet common in Australia). Until same-sex marriage is allowed, LGBTI people who dislike marriage do not have the choice not to marry. Currently, the government makes that decision for them. When we have marriage equality they will be able to put their principles into practice and emphatically reject the institution they disdain. If for no other reason, left wing critics of marriage should fight for marriage equality so that everyone has the right to decide not to wed.

16. Churning the Tasmanian mud: marriage equality and the Tasmanian tipping point

A version of this essay was published in the Griffith Review, *Autumn 2013*

In 2012-13 there was an eruption of national commentary on Tasmania and its future, much of it prejudiced, ignorant and shallow. On the political right the island was portrayed as the kind of poor, tree-hugging, gay-loving, welfare-dependent, enterprise-free society Green-dominated Labor governments inevitably create. These images fitted into a narrative established in colonial times when Tasmania was thought of as a government-subsidised prison society where laziness, pauperism and depravity were rife and self-discipline and self-help unknown. Whether West Australian Premier, Colin Barnett, realised it or not, his attacks on Tasmania's "mendicancy" drew as much strength from ancient fears and stereotypes of Tasmania as a flawed and failed place as from contemporary concerns about the distribution of GST revenues.

The anti-Tasmanian myths perpetuated by progressive intellectuals were less obvious but just as self-serving. Debate on Tasmania was framed in terms of a unique "moment", "watershed" or "tipping point" where the island faced the choice between embracing the creativity and innovation of the elite few or being held back by "local resistance to change" and "stuck in the mud of the past". As with the right's story about Tasmania's poverty and weakness, the cultural left's wipe-the-slate-clean-and-start-again story about Tasmania's future was predicted on the assumption that mainstream Tasmanian politics and society is fundamentally flawed, destined to failure and in need of rescue. It also has a very long pedigree. We were told we were on the cusp of a radical rupture with the past when transportation ended, when the colonies federated, when the first Labor/Green Accord was forged in 1989 and when "the New Tasmania" was born from, among other things, the decriminalisation of homosexuality in 1997. Each time the reality was far more complex. It is an understandable and sometimes charming peculiarity of immigrant societies that we see the past as wholly grim and gone and the future as holding nothing but promise, with an unbridgeable chasm between the two. But it is also a curse. By pretending a historically important event is a repudiation of what has gone before rather than its outgrowth we're destined not to understand or gain from these events. As in a nightmare, the faster we try to run from the past the slower our real progress becomes.

Tasmania's leadership on marriage equality was a good example of how distorted images of Tasmania obscure reality. In August 2012 Premier Lara Giddings announced her government would pass legislation allowing same-sex couples to marry. Continental opinion was bemused. Some commentators labelled it "unlikely" and "ironic" that the last state to decriminalise homosexuality was the first to move on same-sex marriage. People on both sides of the marriage equality debate thought Tasmania was stepping out of type (with the exception of Helen Razor who opposes same-sex marriage as co-option of gay people into an archaic institution. Tasmanian leadership on the issue confirmed her pre-existing stereotype of the island as a "creepy" monstrosity). The reason the nation was so surprised was that Tasmania has always been a convenient screen upon which it can project everything it doesn't like about itself, including its homophobia. For centuries, islands have unwillingly served the psychological role of allowing continental people to exonerate themselves of their own faults. But now Tasmania was defying its set place in the national story. It was inevitable continental commentators would respond by portraying Tasmania's leadership on marriage equality as an exception to the proper order of things.

Of course, such commentary was all nonsense. Tasmania had been on the path to marriage equality for many years. In 2005 it was the first state to see same-sex marriage legislation introduced to parliament and publicly debated, with the Bill re-introduced in 2008 and 2010. In 2003 Tasmania became the first state to have a scheme for formally recognising same-sex relationships and was the first state to officially recognise overseas same-sex marriages in 2010. In 2009 Tasmanian Labor was the first state ALP branch to endorse marriage equality at its state conference and in 2011 the Tasmanian House of Assembly was the first Australian legislative chamber to pass a motion in support of marriage equality. Far from being an unlikely first-mover on marriage equality, Tasmania was on a trajectory to lead the nation on the issue since the mid 2000s.

As confirmation of this trajectory, we only need to look at reforms more broadly. Tasmania's anti-discrimination laws enacted in 1999 are the strongest in the nation with no exemptions allowing religious organisations to directly disadvantage lesbian, gay, bisexual, transgender and intersex (LGBTI) people. These laws have been effectively utilised to launch globally-unprecedented challenges to everything from the gay blood donation ban to the use of LGBTI human rights as wedge issues during elections. Tasmania's recognition of same-sex parenting, the state school system's concerted efforts to challenge classroom homophobia, and the government's funding of lesbian, gay, bisexual and transgender support organisations, have all led where other states have since followed. Beyond these legislative and policy initiatives lie a solid foundation of public support. Polls consistently show support for gay equality is higher in Tasmania than nationally.

But that still leaves unexplained how the last state to decriminalise homosexuality has moved so far so quickly. To understand the depth of Tasmania's transformation it is important to understand how repressive Tasmania once was for homosexuals. Our former laws against gay sex carried the harshest penalties in the western world - 21 years in gaol. They persisted thanks to public support, with polls in the late 1980s showing opposition to decriminalisation to be 15% higher than the national average. Through the Twentieth century our old anti-gay laws were enforced more often than in the other states, with their repressive impact magnified by laws unique to Tasmania criminalising male cross dressing. In the Nineteenth century, unprecedented steps were taken to eliminate same-sex relationships among convicts. These included the separate and silent prison at Port Arthur and the continuation of capital punishment until 1867, long after it had been abandoned elsewhere in the British Empire.

When I came out in 1987 I was immediately made aware of this repressive legacy. At the first gay community meetings I attended I was warned about the police practice of taking down the car registration numbers of those attending such meetings to add to a list of known homosexuals. Not long after that I was horrified to hear then Premier, Robin Gray, declare that homosexuals were not welcome in Tasmania. Only a few months after that the gay rights stall I helped set up at Salamanca Market to gather gay law reform petition signatures was shut down by the Hobart City Council because homosexuals were "not welcome in Hobart's family market". When we defied the ban the police were brought in and, over seven successive Saturdays, 130 people were arrested in what became the largest act of gay rights civil disobedience in Australian history.

The arrests at Salamanca Market bring us back to the question of Tasmania's profound change: the Hobart City Council used the twentieth anniversary of these arrests to apologise and fund a public art work commemorating the event. Both were the first of their kind in Australia. How did this transformation occur? How did Tasmania go from having the worst laws and attitudes on homosexuality to having the best? How, in the words of one American journalist, did Tasmania shift in just a few short years from being Australia's Alabama to its Massachusetts?

The answer lies in the Tasmanian debate over decriminalising homosexuality. It was the most high-profile, bitter and protracted of its kind in Australia. The gay law reform question divided families and communities. The laws themselves drew condemnation from the UN Human Rights Committee, Amnesty International, the Federal Government and the High Court. Angry resistance to reform in the state Upper House and at hateful anti-gay rallies saw Tasmania dubbed "Bigots Island" in the British press and sparked a boycott of Tasmanian produce. The campaigns for and against reform mobilised thousands of people to rally, march, leaflet, write and lobby. Homosexual decriminalisation was rarely out of the news for almost a decade. Gay law reform became a stage upon which the state played out its many tensions and frustrations.

One feature of the debate that accounts for its profound effect was the kind of face-to-face community education not seen on such a systematic basis in Australia until then. For almost a decade, ordinary LGBTI Tasmanians travelled around the state addressing church groups, Rotary Clubs and party branch meetings about their everyday experiences and how the law affected them. The change which accumulates from this kind of community education is magnified in an interconnected community like Tasmania's. When historians come to ask how it was that Tasmanians embraced ground-breaking gay law reforms they will conclude that it was often the quietest voices which spoke the loudest.

High profile actions also had a role to play. In early 1994 the UN Human Rights Committee's condemnation of the Tasmanian laws sparked a national debate which quickly turned to the question of whether the Federal

Government had the power to override the offending Tasmanian statutes. To bring it back to the core issue of gay equality several gay men, including my then partner and I, decided to turn ourselves into the police with statutory declarations outlining our illegal sexual activity. I still recall the odd questions the police asked me in my interview – how often had this occurred with the co-accused and at what addresses, how did I get from position A to position B and what was I wearing at the time? Only later did I realise these were typically questions asked of anyone who had confessed to a serious crime, be it armed robbery, rape, murder or homosexuality. At that moment I realised what a farce our old laws really were. As it happened the police did not arrest us despite having the evidence they needed. That decision, as much as any other, destroyed the credibility of our discriminatory old laws and those who continued to defend them.

Another important legacy of the decriminalisation debate was the decision of LGBTI people to stay in or move to Tasmania. As I've noted in previous chapters, the demographic shift of LGBTI people out of inner-city ghettoes and towards suburban and regional areas, drawn by growing tolerance in these areas, is an accelerating trend across the western world. But in Tasmania it was sudden and dramatic. Before the decriminalisation debate it was common for LGBTI people to leave the state if they wished to lead an open life. After decriminalisation that trend was reversed with successive censuses recording unparalleled growth in the number of same-sex couples living in Tasmania. The significance of this demographic shift lies in the fact nothing changes attitudes towards same-sex relationships as quickly or as profoundly as familiarity. When heterosexual people can see that same-sex partners conduct their lives and relationships the same as everyone else it becomes much harder to justify legal discrimination against these relationships (for more on this see chapter 11).

But if there was one legacy of the decriminalisation debate which has contributed more than any other to the situation we have today it is this: In the course of that debate Tasmanians witnessed some of the worst anti-gay bigotry seen in modern Australian history. They saw first-hand the damage caused by prejudice and discrimination. They experienced how hate divides and cripples entire communities. And having seen all this they opted instead for a society based on tolerance and inclusion.

Taking all this into account it becomes clear Tasmania's progress towards marriage equality was not despite our history, but because of it. Far from resisting change, the mass of ordinary Tasmanians were at its cutting edge. The mud of Tasmania's past is not something to be shaken from our boots. Our capacity for reform springs from that mud, just as we have done. And it is all the more precious for that.

Of course, there are other reasons Tasmania led the way on marriage equality. Just as Tasmania's leadership on the issue has been the logical outcome of a long narrative about the place of sexual minorities in Tasmanian society, so it was also the result of a long narrative about Tasmania's place in the federation. Tasmania's leading federalist Andrew Inglis-Clarke, like his hero Giuseppe Mazzini, was a romantic nationalist who hoped Tasmania would be elevated by federalism. In 2012 and 2013 it felt the opposite. It felt like Tasmania was badly governed from Capitol Hill. State revenues from Canberra were hit by the global financial crisis and our exports and tourism were down thanks to the over-valuation of the dollar by the mining boom. Our agricultural products were under threat from cheap foreign imports and the diseases they carry. National policy on key social issues like marriage equality was being directed not by the majority but by a handful of socially-conservative seats in Western Sydney. Meanwhile, initiatives like the globally-acclaimed Museum of Old and New Art fostered an image of Tasmania as creative and innovative. There was a sense in Tasmania that we needed to assert ourselves more within the federal system, and blaze our own trail to economic and cultural development. Taking the lead on marriage equality, in defiance of Canberra, sat well in this narrative of greater Tasmanian autonomy.

Apart from marriage equality there were many other cases of real change arising from within Tasmania's past and its people rather than from outside them. The island's world-leading environment movement is the obvious example. The dauntless Aboriginal movement is another. The island's radical artistic and literary scene is yet another. What these political and cultural phenomena share with the island's campaign for LGBTI equality is that the determination and risk-taking that has led to their success was forged by the strident adversity and repression they have too often faced. In turn, that adversity has grown stronger because of the challenge presented to it by those seeking change, and so around it goes. Tasmania is a fractured and polarised society with a weak middle ground. It moves forward by the grinding of these fault lines against each other, unfortunately sometimes producing great heat and instability, but offering far more to the world as a result. Tasmania is neither entirely conservative nor predictably progressive. If it were, it could not have made its great and original contribution to the nation and the world. Tasmania is both the abominable Fatal Shore and the felicitous Apple Isle, together at the same time. The fact that such a paradox can exist in the heart of a single people and place is not easy to grasp. But without at least attempting to grapple with it Tasmania remains impossible to explain.

So it is to marriage equality we return. In September 2012, after the triumphant passage of the Same-Sex Marriage Bill through the House of Assembly, followed by weeks of hard-fought marriage equality campaigning of an intensity not seen in Australia before, the Tasmanian Upper House narrowly defeated marriage equality down by just two votes. Before the vote, momentum was strong with support emerging from all sections of the community. It really felt like reform was achievable with pro-equality endorsements coming from prominent legal academics, economists, mental health experts and celebrities, and with a tide of popular support that saw Upper House members drowned by thousands of pro-equality emails and petitioners. But in the end Upper House support melted away. Those Upper House members whose votes were needed to pass the Bill justified their failure to support it with concerns about the risk and cost of a potential

High Court challenge (for more on the constitutionality of state same-sex marriage laws see chapter 12). These concerns were wildly exaggerated leading some people to see them as camouflage for homophobic prejudice. I'm not so sure. I heard in the voices of the faltering MPs a loss of nerve. They talked about how often Tasmania had lost in the High Court in the past, but they were expressing something much deeper and more insidious - the belief I've already cited that Tasmania is flawed at its core and that Tasmanians are born to fail. A desperate desire to prove to ourselves we can succeed and a fatal fear that we never will: these two contradictory and interdependent impulses drove and sank Tasmania's bid to become the first place in Australia to allow same-sex marriages.

Tasmania's leadership on marriage equality opened up the opportunity for other states and territories to act. The ACT Government faced none of the parliamentary or psychological barriers that inhibit Tasmania. Its single chamber assembly enacted marriage equality legislation in 2013. Unfortunately, the ACT law was poorly framed. Unlike Tasmania's legislation, the ACT's impinged on the definition of marriage from the federal Marriage Act. As predicted by constitutional experts, the ACT law was struck down by the High Court. But still, the ACT law moved marriage equality forward by allowing thirty-one same-sex couples to become the first to marry under an Australian statute. Should federal parliament again fail to pass marriage equality, the issue will inevitably return to the states. Legislation similar to Tasmania's has a chance of passing in South Australia and NSW thanks to Liberal Party conscience votes in both states. The Tasmanian campaign is also far from over. In typical fashion, the polarised nature of the Tasmanian debate, with its see-sawing hopes and disappointments, has hardened the resolve of those campaigning for and against reform. Those against are determined the issue will not be re-visited. Those for are just as determined the legislation will be passed.

Our battle will be one for same-sex equality and dignity. But it will also be a battle for the Tasmanian soul, as all our battles have always been. The world may watch as it sometimes does, or it may ignore us, as is more often the case. But we shall churn the Tasmanian mud regardless, until something truly remarkable again springs forth.

ENDNOTES

1. Wolfson, E., *Why Marriage Matters; America, Equality and Gay People's Right to Marry*, Simon and Schuster, New York, 2004, p18

2. Argent, S., 'I am the mother of one equal and one unequal son", Mamamia website, 23.4.2013, http://www.mamamia.com.au/news/shelly-argent-i-am-the-mother-of-one-equal-and-one-unequal-son/

3. Barbeau v British Columbia (Attorney General), 2003 BCCA 251 at 156, also Ontario Court of Appeal, Halpern v Canada (2003).

4. The final report of the Senate Legal and Constitutional Affairs Committee inquiry into the Marriage Equality Amendment Bill 2009, as well as a selection of the submissions to that inquiry, can be found at http://www.aph.gov.au/Senate/committee/legcon_ctte/marriage_equality/index.htm. Some of the extracts reproduced here are from submissions not posted to the Senate website, or otherwise not publicly available. Written permission has been obtained from all submission writers for the use of their extracts and their names.

5. Tegg, J., Letter to the editor, Hobart Mercury, 2011

6. For workplace discrimination see, *The Pink Ceiling is Too Low: workplace experiences of lesbians, gay men and transgender people*. NSW Gay and Lesbian Rights Lobby, 1999, http://glrl.org.au/images/stories/the_pink_ceiling_is_too_low.pdf.
For hate crime see Mason, G., *Violence against lesbians and gay men*. Australian Institute for Criminology, 1993, http://www.aic.gov.au/documents/D/2/2/{D22F8857-A477-4BA0-BAB8-5C04C2B1E7E9}vpt2.pdf

7. For more on health risk in young people see *Writing Themselves in Again, the 2nd national report on the sexual health and wellbeing of same-sex attracted young people*. Australian Centre for Sex, Health and Society, http://www.glhv.org.au/files/writing_themselves_in_again.pdf

8. Herdt, G., and R Kertzner, "I Do, but I Can't: The Impact of Marriage Denial on the Mental Health and Sexual Citizenship of Lesbians and Gay Men in the United States", *Journal of the National Sexual Research Centre*, Issue 1, Vol 3, 2006, pp.33-49.

9. Dane, S., B. Masser, and J. Duck, *Not So Private Lives: National Findings on the Relationships and Well-Being of Same-Sex Attracted Australians*. The University of Queensland, 2009. See: http://www.not-soprivatelives.com/Not-So-Private- Lives-Relationship-Recognition-Report-Aug-2009_F4.pdf

10. Goodridge v Dept. of Public Health, 798 N.E.2d 941 (Mass. 2003).

[11] Leyonhjelm, D., "Aim of same-sex marriage bill is to get government out of the bedroom", *The Canberra Times*, 25.3.2015, http://www.canberratimes.com.au/comment/aim-of-samesex-marriage-bill-is-to-get-government-out-of-the-bedroom-20150325-1m74j0.html

[12] Carson, C., R. Luker and P. A. Russell (eds), (2000) *The Papers of Martin Luther King, Jr: Symbol of the Movement*, January 1957, University of California Press, Berkeley. Page 436.

[13] Arendt, H. and P. A. Baeher (ed), *The portable Hannah Arendt*, Penguin, New York, 2000, p. 236. 7 Loving v Virginia (1967) 388 U.S. 1

[14] Loving v Virginia (1967) 388 U.S. 1

[15] Croome, R., "True and Good Citizens", *Overland*, 203, Winter 2011

[16] Petition of the "half-caste" women of Broome, January 1935 to the President and Members of the Western Australian Royal Commission to inquire into allegations of the mistreatment of Aborigines, reproduced in Attwood, B., and A Markus, *The struggle for Aboriginal Rights: a documentary history*, Allen and Unwin, 1999

[17] Loving, M., *Loving for All*, June 12, 2007. http://www.freedomtomarry.org/pdfs/mildred_loving-statement.pdf

[18] Together with the dates when marriage equality was achieved, the nations where same-sex couples can marry (as at May 31st 2015) are, the Netherlands (2001), Belgium (2003), Canada (provincially beginning in 2003, nationally in 2005), Spain (2005), South Africa (2006), Nor- way (2009) Sweden (2009), Portugal (2010), Iceland (2010), Argen- tina (2010), Denmark (2012), Brasil (2013), Uruguay (2013), France (2013), New Zealand (2013), UK (2014), Finland (2015), Luxembourg (2015), Ireland (2015). In the US, same-sex marriage is allowed in 36 states and the District of Columbia. Some Mexican states also allow same- sex marriages.

[19] In the time it took to write the original version of this text in 2010, marriage equality was achieved in eight of the jurisdictions mentioned above. Since then another thirteen countries and 31 US states have joined the list.

[20] In its submission to the 2009 Senate inquiry into the Marriage Equality Amendment Bill, Australian Marriage Equality estimated that "between 3000 and 4000 Australian couples have married overseas". According to AME, this estimate was based on "the numbers of couples who have contacted us for advice, and the numbers who have entered into British civil partnerships in UK consulates in Australia. Mostly these couples have married in countries without residency requirements for marriage, such as Canada (we estimate the number of Australian couples who have entered into Canadian same-sex marriages to be about 2000). But we have been contacted by couples who have married in all the nations which allow same-sex marriage."

21 Dane, S., B. Masser, and J. Duck, *Not So Private Lives, op cit*

22 Rosenbaum, A., "Gay marriage in Australia: Married but not wed", *The Age*, 28.02.2015, http://www.smh.com.au/national/gay-marriage-in-australia-married-but-not-wed-20150227-13o6s2.html

23 "Let them wed", *The Economist*, January 4, 1996. Available at http://www.economist.com/PrinterFriendly.cfm?Story_ID=2515389

24 APS endorses APA marriage equality statement, 22.12.11, http://www.psychology.org.au/Newsandupdates/22Dec2011/
APA re-iterates support for same-sex marriage, 11.8.10, http://www.apa.org/news/press/releases/2010/08/support-same-sex-marriage.aspx
Headspace submission to the 2012 Senate inquiry into marriage equality, http://www.headspace.org.au/media/516781/sub%20197_headspace.pdf

25 Riggs, D., quoted in "APS endorses APA marriage equality resolution", Australian Psychological Society, 22.12.11, http://www.psychology.org.au/Newsandupdates/22Dec2011/

26 http://www.australianmarriageequality.org/who-supports-equality/civil-leaders/

27 Spedale D., and W. Eskridge, *Gay Marriage: For Better or Worse? What We've Learnt from the Evidence.* Oxford University Press, 2006

28 Wright, R.G., "Same-sex legal marriage and psychological well-being: findings from the California health interview survey", American Journal of Public Health: February 2013, Vol. 103, No. 2, pp. 339-346

29 "Marriage the key to middle aged happiness", *Australian Financial Review*, 10.02.2015, http://www.afr.com/p/lifestyle/marriage_the_key_to_middle_age_happiness_KO7mR9oabN2sBcWMpIjsZI

30 "Marriage equality and LGBT health", American Psychological Society, 2010, http://www.apa.org/about/gr/issues/lgbt/marriage-equality.pdf

31 Ducharme, J. K., et al, "Does the 'marriage benefit' extend to same-sex unions: evidence from a sample of married lesbian couples in Massachusetts", Journal of Homosexuality, Vol 59, Issue 4, 2012

32 MacIntosh, H., etc al, Same-sex marriage in Canada: The impact of legal marriage on the first cohort of gay and lesbian Canadians to wed, Canadian Journal of Human Sexuality, Vol 19 (3), 2010

33 "NYC Same-Sex Marriages Generate $259 Million in Economic Impact", July 24th, 2012, http://www.mikebloomberg.com/index.cfm?-objectid=B9BB6B4E-C29C-7CA2-F1D74B44ADE35CC4

[34] Williams Institute, UCLA, The Business Impact of Opening Marriage to Same-sex Couples, http://williamsinstitute.law.ucla.edu/interactive-economic-impact/

[35] Australian Bureau of Statistics, "Australian Social Trends, Same-Sex Couples", July 2013, http://www.abs.gov.au/AUSSTATS/abs@.nsf/Lookup/4102.0Main+Features10July+2013#number

[36] Australian Securities and Investment Commission, "How Much Does a Wedding Cost?", https://www.moneysmart.gov.au/managing-your-money/budgeting/simple-ways-to-save-money/how-much-can-a-wedding-cost

[37] Gay and Lesbian Tourism Australia, "Australia overlooked on LGBT holiday wish-lists", media release, 11.05.2015

[38] Greig, B., Banning gay marriage impacts on skilled migration, *Sydney Morning Herald*, 18.5.2013, http://www.smh.com.au/comment/banning-gay-marriage-impacts-on-skilled-migration-20130518-2jt27.html

[39] Diversity Council of Australia, "Diversity Council of Australia backs marriage equality", media release, 01.04.2015

[40] Nicholson, R., "Allens says same-sex marriage is just good business", Australian Financial Review, 15.05.2015, http://www.afr.com/business/legal/allens-says-samesex-marriage-is-just-good-business-20150514-gh-1cxh

[41] Ridout, H., quoted in Karvelas, P., "Heather Ridout speaks in support of same-sex partnerships", *The Australian*, 29.10.2010, http://www.theaustralian.com.au/national-affairs/heather-ridout-speaks-in-support-of-same-sex-partnerships/story-fn59niix-1225962385273

[42] Calandrino, M., *Sexual Orientation Discrimination in the UK Labour Market*. St Anthony's College, University of Oxford, 1999.

[43] Berg, C., "If marriage is so good why not invite everyone in", The Age, 21.11.10, http://www.theage.com.au/it-pro/if-marriage-is-so-good-why-not-invite-everyone-in-20101120-18tu.html

[44] 'Q&A: Amanda Vanstone on why conservatives should support marriage equality', 7 March 2012, *Australian Marriage Equality*. http://www.australianmarriageequality.com/wp/2012/03/07/qa-amanda-vanstone-on-why-conservatives-should-support-marriage-equality/

[45] Badgett, M.V., N. Goldberg and C. Ramos, *The Effects of Marriage Equality in Massachusetts: A survey of the experiences and impact of marriage on same-sex couples*. UCLA School of Law, 2009. Also, *When Gay People Get Married: What Happens When Societies Legalize Same-Sex Marriage*. New York University Press, 2009, 19

46   Not her real name, at her request.

47   "The Times backs gay marriage" Leader Article, *The Times*, 5.3.2012

48   For a summary of the relevant Scandinavian statistics see, MV Lee Badgett, "Prenuptial Jitters: Did gay marriage destroy heterosexual marriage in Scandinavia?", *Slate* magazine, May 2004, See: http://www.slate.com/id/2100884/

49   For more, see http://www.cdc.gov/nchs/data/nvss/Divorce%20Rates%2090%20 95%20and%2099-07.pdf

50   For more see N. Silver, "Divorce Rates Higher in States with Gay Marriage Bans", 2010, in *FiveThirtyEight.com*. See: http://www.fivethirtyeight. com/2010/01/divorce-rates-appear-higher-in-states.html

51   Spedale, D. R., and W. N. Eskridge Jr, "The Hitch", *The Wall Street Journal*, 27 October 2006. Available at http://online.wsj.com/article/ SB116191428485605594.html

52   Rubin, R., "Conservatives filing brief in favor of gay marriage", *Washington Post*, 3.3.2015 http://www.washingtonpost.com/blogs/right-turn/wp/2015/03/03/conservatives-filing-brief-in-favor-of-gay-marriage/

53   Shortall, J., What Gay Marriage Advocates Aren't Telling You, Huffington Post, 24.02.2015, http://www.huffingtonpost.co.uk/jessica-shortall/ gay-marriage-advocates_b_6738198.html

54   ibid, p1 & 4

55   For an overview of same-sex relationships in different historical and cultural contexts see W N Eskridge, The Case for Same-Sex Marriage, pp 15-51

56   Other work in this field includes recent research into "affrèrements", legal, marriage-like contracts between same sex and other partners in late mediaeval France (http://www.sciencedaily.com/releases/2007/08/070823110231.htm)

57   http://www.aaanet.org/issues/policy-advocacy/Statement-on-Marriage-and-the-Family.cfm

58   Herek G.M., "Legal recognition of same-sex relationships in the United States: a social science perspective", *American Psychologist*, No 6, Vol 6, pp. 607-621, see p. 609ff. Also see, Weedon-Fekjr, H., "The demographics of same-sex marriages in Norway and Sweden", *Demography*, Feb, 2006.

59   Studies like the Gay Community Periodic Surveys and the Sydney Men and health study deliberately draw their sample from gay and bisexual men who attend inner-urban bars, STI clinics and sex clubs, because

the researchers are specifically looking at what causes HIV infection risk and how to reduce that risk. Prominent Australian sexual health researcher, Professor Anne Mitchell, has explained why so many studies focus on those gay men who have high numbers of sexual partners. *"... the research, particularly the research done in Australia, is all funded with HIV prevention money and therefore it is very directed at being able to recruit the people who may be at risk of HIV....But it doesn't take account of the much wider gay community who is not of interest to social researchers because they are not at any risk of HIV. They are just living their lives in suburbia as monogamous couples with no sorties out to the gay saunas or anything at the weekend and they are no more at HIV risk than any other person in the community, in fact less than a lot of heterosexuals I would suspect.(* T79, Cain v Australian Red Cross Blood Service, Tasmanian Anti-Discrimination Tribunal, 2008)

[60] Xiridou M., R. Geskus, J. de Wit, R. Coutinho, M. Kretzschmar, "The contribution of steady and casual partnerships to the incidence of HIV infection among homosexual men in Amsterdam", *AIDS*, Issue 7, Vol 17, May 2003, pp. 1029-1038, See: http://journals.lww.com/aidsonline/pages/articleviewer.aspx?-year=2003andissue=05020andarticle=00012andtype=f ulltext. An analysis of the misuse of this study by opponents of same-sex marriage is available at http://www.boxturtlebulletin.com/Articles/000,003.htm

[61] For example: Bradford, J., C. Ryan, and E. Rothblum, "National lesbian healthcare survey: Implications for mental health", *Journal of Consulting and Clinical Psychology*, Vol 62 No 2, 1994, pp. 228-242. Falkner, A., and J. Garber, *2001 gay/lesbian consumer online census*. Syracuse, Syracuse University, New York, OpusComm, and GSociety. 2002 Morris, J., K. Balsam, K., and E. Rothblum, (2002). "Lesbian and bisexual mothers and nonmothers: Demographics and the coming-out process", *Developmental Psychology*, 16, 144156. Blumstein, P., and P. Schwartz, *American couples: Money, work, sex*. William Morrow, New York, 1983 Bryant, A. S., "Relationship characteristics of gay and lesbian couples: Findings from a national survey", *Journal of Gay and Lesbian Social Services*, 1, 1994, pp. 101-117. Kurdek, L. A., "Differences between gay and lesbian cohabiting couples", *Journal of Social Personal Relationships*, 20, 2003, pp. 411-436. Peplau, L. A., and K. P. Beals, "The family lives of lesbians and gay men", in A. L. Vangelisti (Ed.), *Handbook of family communication*, pp. 233-248, 2004 Peplau, L. and L. Spalding, "The close relationships of lesbians, gay men and bisexuals", in C. Hendrick and S. Hendrick (Eds.). *Close relationships: A sourcebook*. Thousand Oaks, California Sage, 2000, pp. 449-474.

[62] The authors of the Vermont study agreed with Professor Mitchell, that most previous studies were of gays and lesbians "who are visible and concentrated", producing *a body of literature about homosexual lives that tends toward the 'exceptional'"* (see, Elder, G., "The Non-significance of Significant Others: a National Geography of Gay and Lesbian Coupledom", report from the University of Vermont, http://www.newswise.com/articles/view/518987/)

[63] Rosenfeld, S., "Couple Longevity in the Era of Same-Sex Marriage in the U.S.", *Journal of Marriage and Family*, October 2014.

[64] Gottlieb, S., "Five years of gay marriage", *Radio Nederland Wereldom-roep*, 2006. See: http://static.rnw.nl/migratie/www.radionetherlands.nl/currentaffairs/gay060403-redirected

[65] Badgett, MV Lee, Recognition for same-sex couples: divorce and terminations", Williams Institute, UCLA, December 2014, http://williamsinstitute.law.ucla.edu/wp-content/uploads/Badgett-Mallory-Divorce-Terminations-Dec-2014.pdf. For a news report see: http://www.advocate.com/politics/marriage-equality/2014/12/13/report-same-sex-couples-less-likely-divorce

[66] In 2012 Coalition Government minister and conservative Catholic, Kevin Andrews, wrote a 500 page book arguing "marriage is an optimal relationship for the psychological, emotional and physical wellbeing of adults and children" and "the bedrock of successful societies", yet he is one of the most influential opponents of same-sex couples marrying. Andrews, K., *Maybe 'I do': modern marriage and the pursuit of happiness*, Connor Court, Ballan, Australia, 2012, p1

[67] d'Ancona, Matthew. "The case for gay marriage is fundamentally conservative - it will strengthen Britain's social fabric", *The Telegraph (UK)*, 10 March 2012.

[68] http://www.smh.com.au/rugby-union/wallaby-boycotts-marriage-until-gays-have-same-right-20111126-1o0b0.html

[69] In an article about the 2009 Australian Labor Party National Conference decision not to allow same-sex marriage, the Australian Christian Lobby Managing Director, Jim Wallace stated, "The line was held by the personal commitment of Prime Minister Kevin Rudd to the election promises he had made, as a reflection of his personal faith." See: http://www.acl.org.au/pdfs/load_pdf_public.pdf?pdf_id=1369and-from=NATIONAL

[70] See http://www.highbeam.com/doc/1P1-77144847.html

[71] "Non-Christians to marry in Anglican churches, *The Australian*, 20.10.2009, http://www.theaustralian.com.au/archive/news/non-christians-to-marry-in-anglican-churches/story-e6frg6o6-1225788552076

72 Boswell, J., *Same-sex unions in pre-modern Europe*. Random House, New York, 1994

73 Australian Institute of Family Studies, "Family Facts and Figures: Marriage", 2012, https://aifs.gov.au/institute/info/charts/marriage/index. htm ame=Summaryandprodno=3310.0andissue=2008andnum=andview=

74 Heard, J., "Aisle of Plenty" *The Spectator Australia* 20 February 2013 accessible at http://bit.ly/1wqAlRl

75 McRae, J., "Normal part of the community", *The Mercury*, 6.4.2015, p13

76 Australian Bureau of Statistics, *Couples in Australia*. See Doc no 4102.0, http://www.abs.gov.au/AUSSTATS/abs@.nsf/Lookup/4102.0Main+-Features20March%202009

77 Millbank, J., *Meet the Parents: A Review of the Research on Lesbian and Gay Families*. NSW Gay and Lesbian Rights Lobby, Sydney, 2002. See: http://glrl.org.au/images/stories/meet_the_parents.pdf

78 Dane, *op cit.* 37 Wallace, J., "Should we legalise gay marriage?", *Examiner*, 4 September 2009, p. 23.

79 Wallace, J., "Should we legalise gay marriage?", *Examiner*, 4 September 2009, p23.

80 Van Gend, D., "Saying sorry means not doing it again", *Online Opinion*, 23.03.2015, http://www.onlineopinion.com.au/view.asp?article=17197&page=0

81 Shelton, L., "Rudd's change on marriage sets up a new stolen generation", Australian Christian Lobby media release, 21.5.2013

82 Minniecon, R., "Stolen generation advocates call for Christian Lobby apology for 'disrespectful' and 'dehumanizing' marriage equality comments, Kinchela Boys Home media release, 21.5.2013

83 Short, E., D Riggs, A. Perlesz, R. Brown and G. Kane, *Lesbian, Gay, Bisexual and Transgender (LGBT) Parented Families: a literature review prepared for The Australian Psychological Society*. Melbourne, 2007. See: http://www.psychology.org.au/Assets/Files/LGBT-Families-Lit-Review.pdf
Also see McNair, R., *Outcomes for Children Born of ART in a Diverse Range of Families*. (Occasional Paper), Melbourne: Victorian Law Reform Commission, 2004.
Hastings, P., J. Vyncke, C. Sullivan, K. McShane, M. Benibgui and W. Utendale, *Children's Development of Social Competence Across Family Types*. Canada: Department of Justice, 2006
Patterson, C., *Lesbian and Gay Parenting*. Washington: American Psychological Association, 2005.

[84] http://www.healthychildren.org/English/family-life/family-dynamics/
      types-of-families/pages/Gay-and-Lesbian-Parents.aspx

[85] Patterson, CJ, Lesbian & Gay Parents & Their Children: Summary Of
      Research Findings, http://www.apa.org/pi/lgbt/resources/parenting.
      aspx#

[86] ibid

[87] ibid

[88] Crouch, S., et al, "Parent-reported measures of child health and
      wellbeing in same-sex parent families: a cross-sectional survey", *BMC
      Public Health* 2014, 14:635, For a summary by the author, see: http://
      theconversation.com/kids-from-same-sex-families-fare-as-well-as-peers-
      or-better-28803

[89] Parkinson, P. (2011) "For Kids' Sake: Repairing the social environment
      for Australian children and young people". *The University of Sydney*,
      http://sydney.edu.au/law/news/docs_pdfs_images/2011/Sep/FKS-Re-
      searchReport.pdf

[90] Shanahan, A. "Children suffer under political correctness", *The
      Australian,* 3 September 2011. http://www.theaustralian.com.au/
      news/opinion/children-suffer-under-political-correctness/story-e6frg-
      6zo-1226127876896

[91] Jensen, E. "Age of the Amateur with reason in retreat", *Sydney Morning
      Herald.* 4 January 2012. http://www.smh.com.au/opinion/politics/
      age-of-the-amateur-with-reason-in-retreat-20120103-1pjd7.html,
      Croome, R. "Parkinson report an argument for same-sex marriage",
      ABC The Drum Unleashed. 14 September 2011. http://www.abc.net.au/
      unleashed/2897380.html

[92] For more see, http://www.abc.net.au/news/2011-09-14/croome-parkin-
      son-report-an-argument-for-same-sex-marriage/2897380, and http://
      www.starobserver.com.au/news/parkinson-report-not-about-gay-par-
      ents/61599

[93] For more see, http://www.nytimes.com/2012/10/13/us/mark-regnerus-
      and-the-role-of-faith-in-academics.html?_r=0, and http://articles.
      latimes.com/2012/jun/13/opinion/la-oe-frank-same-sex-regnerus-fami-
      ly-20120613

[94] Akerman, P., "When convenience and distraction unite", *Daily Tele-
      graph,* 3 August 2009. See: http://blogs.news.com.au/dailytelegraph/
      piersakerman/index.php/dailytelegraph/comments/when_conve-
      nience_a nd_distraction_unite/

[95] Plato, *Symposium.* See translation by Alexander Nehamas and Paul
      Woodruff at p.28

[96] Abbott, T., "Not for Adam and Steve," 9 May 2008 on *ABC*. See: http://www.abc.net.au/unleashed/stories/s2240035.htm

[97] "More mature marriage debate needed", Australian Christian Lobby media release, 15.07.2014, http://www.acl.org.au/2014/07/mr-more-mature-marriage-debate-needed/

[98] Australian Christian Lobby, "Submission to the Legal and Constitutional Affairs Legislation Committee Concerning the Recognition of Foreign Marriages Bill 2014"

[99] Editorial, *Boston Globe*, "Ads mislead voters about same-sex marriage in Mass. Schools", 03.11.2012, http://www.bostonglobe.com/opinion/editorials/2012/11/02/maine-and-elsewhere-ads-mislead-voters-about-same-sex-marriage-massachusetts-schools/Q1rm2BfFjczRYHsP4WS-M7L/story.html

[100] "Danish vote to force church to marry homosexuals shows", Australian Christian Lobby media release, 8.6.2012, http://www.acl.org.au/2012/06/mr-danish-vote-to-force-church-to-marry-homosexuals-shows-our-politicians-naive-to-accept-activists%E2%80%99-assurances/

[101] Byrne Patrick, "Same-sex marriage: is it harmless?", News Weekly, 12.10.2013, http://www.acl.org.au/2013/10/same-sex-marriage-is-it-harmless/

[102] Moss, C., *The myth of persecution: how early Christians invented the story of martyrdom*, Harper Collins, New York, 2013

[103] Cooper, K., Professor of Ancient History, University of Manchester, in Michael Scott, "Jesus Rise to Power", episode 3

[104] Moss, op cit, p249-256

[105] O'Neill, Brendan, "I now pronounce you partner 1 and partner 2", *The Australian*, 2012, http://www.theaustralian.com.au/national-affairs/opinion/i-now-pronounce-you-partner-1-and-partner-2-why-gay-marriage-is-bad-for-us-all/story-e6frgd0x-1226320722485

[106] George Wallace quoted in RC Snyder, *Gay Marriage and Democracy*, p 114

[107] O'Neill, op cit

[108] O'Neill Brendan, "Gay marriage and the death of freedom", *The Spectator*, 6.12.2014, http://www.spectator.co.uk/australia/australia-features/9390702/gay-marriage-and-the-death-of-freedom/

[109] "Huge gay marriage protest turns violent in Paris", *The Independent*, 26.05.2013, http://www.independent.co.uk/news/world/europe/france-huge-gay-marriage-protest-turns-violent-in-paris-8632878.html

[110] In the same article O'Neill also refers to a case where an English couple, Tony and Barrie Drewitt-Barlow, have launched a court challenge against the ban on church same-sex marriages in that country. Such a challenge is their right, as it is the church's right to defend its ban. But the challenge is unlikely to succeed given church weddings are so strongly prohibited under English law.

[111] Leyonhjelm, D., "Aim of same-sex marriage bill is to get government out of the bedroom", http://www.smh.com.au/comment/aim-of-samesex-marriage-bill-is-to-get-government-out-of-the-bedroom-20150325-1m74j0.html

[112] Zwartz, B., "Pastor supporter of gay marriage out in the cold", *The Age*, 6.12.2011, http://www.theage.com.au/victoria/pastor-supporter-of-gay-marriage-out-in-the-cold-20111205-1ofht.html

[113] "Liberal Senator Cory Bernardi reignites same-sex controversy", News.com, 18.6.2013, http://www.news.com.au/national/liberal-senator-cory-bernardi-reignites-samesex-controversy/story-fncynjr2-1226665658067

[114] Bolt, Andrew, "Gay marriage push is a slippery slope", Herald Sun, 5.12.2011, http://www.heraldsun.com.au/news/opinion/gay-marriage-push-is-a-slippery-slope/story-e6frfhqf-1226213562479, and "If Leyonhjelm is a true libertarian, why not allow polygamy, too?", Herald Sun, 15.6.2014, http://blogs.news.com.au/heraldsun/andrewbolt/index.php/heraldsun/comments/if_leyonhjelm_is_a_true_libertarian_why_not_allow_polygamy_too/

[115] Among the dozens of jurisdictions that have marriage equality, with a combined population of hundreds of millions of people, there is a solitary example from the Netherlands where one man and two women entered a so-called "cohabitation agreement". Such legal agreements are peculiar to Dutch law, where never intended to allow polygamy and long predate marriage equality. Furthermore, the relationship was a heterosexual one. If this example illustrates any kind of slippery slope to polygamy, it is a slope that starts with heterosexual marriage.

[116] Bolt, Stephanie, "Bolt: I want marriage equality for all", *Crikey*, 13.12.2011, http://www.crikey.com.au/2011/12/13/bolt-i-want-marriage-equality-for-all/

[117] "Supplementary Submission to the Senate Inquiry into the Marriage Equality Amendment Bill 2009 from the Reverend Nathan Nettleton", 18 November 2009, page 6. See: http://www.aph.gov.au/Senate/committee/legcon_ctte/marriage_equality/submissions/sublist3/for/Sub_ef44a.pdf

[118] See, Gavin, F., *Civil Partnerships - Another Year On*. Village Citizens Advice Bureau, 2007. See: http://www.thevillage.org.uk/research/CP_Report/index.html. Also, *Report of the Vermont Commission on Family Recognition and Protection*, April 2008. See: http://www.leg.state.vt.us/WorkGroups/FamilyCommission/VCFRP_Report.pdf

[119] *Report of the New Jersey Civil Union Review Commission*, pp. 10-11. See: http://www.nj.gov/oag/dcr/downloads/CURC-Final-Report-.pdf

[120] Cited in Wolfson, *op cit.*, p134

[121] 46 Goodridge v Dept. of Public Health, *op cit.*

[122] Cox, B. J., "But Why Not Marriage: An Essay on Vermont's Civil Unions Law, Same-Sex Marriage, and Separate but (Un)Equal", 25 Vt. L. Rev. 113 (2000-2001). See also, http://heinonline.org/HOL/LandingPage?collection=journalsandhandle=hein.journals/vlr25anddiv=13andid=andpage=

[123] *Report of the New Jersey Civil Union Review Commission*, pp. 11 and 9. See: http://www.nj.gov/oag/dcr/downloads/CURC-Final-Report-.pdf

[124] Bolt, Stephanie, "Bolt: I want marriage equality for all", *Crikey*, 13.12.2011, http://www.crikey.com.au/2011/12/13/bolt-i-want-marriage-equality-for-all/

[125] Gates G.J., M. V. L. Badgett, D. Ho, *Marriage, registration and dissolution by same-sex couples in the U.S.* The Williams Institute, July 2008. See: http://www.law.ucla.edu/WilliamsInstitute/publications/Couples%20Marr%20Regis%20Diss.pdf

[126] Dane, *op cit.*

[127] Peron, J., Gay Hero of Sydney Hostage Crisis Died a Second Class Citizen, Huffington Post, 16.12.2014, http://www.huffingtonpost.com/james-peron/gay-hero-of-sydney-hostag_b_6332038.html

[128] For more on these polls and responses to them see the following: http://tasmaniantimes.com/index.php?/pr-article/same-sex-marriage-least-important/, http://tasmaniantimes.com/index.php/article/When-it-comes-to-marriage-equality-the-Liberals

[129] For more see, http://www.brisbanetimes.com.au/queensland/christian-lobby-analysis-reveals-strong-gay-focus-20120608-2017g.html

[130] Pitman, T., "Gay marriage - which side of history is Labor on?" *The Punch*, 3 August 2008. Quote amended with Tony Pitman's consent. See: http://www.thepunch.com.au/articles/Gay-marriage-which-side-of-history-is-Labor- on/desc/

[131] See notes 11 and 12, above

[132] "Gay marriage is 'a step too far', says defence minister as Cameron proposes full marriage rights for same-sex couples", *Daily Mail (UK)*,

7 October 2011. http://www.dailymail.co.uk/news/article-2046445/
Gay-marriage-David-Cameron-proposes-marriage-rights-sex-couples.
html

[133] For a list visit http://www.australianmarriageequality.com/employers.
htm

[134] A copy of the ABS announcement can be found at: http://www.austra-lianmarriageequality.com/releases/20090507.htm

[135] A copy of this poll can be found at http://www.newspoll.com.au/im-age_uploads/cgi-lib.17497.1.0601_gay.pdf

[136] For more on this poll, see: Misha Schubert, "Public backs gay unions,
equality", *The Age,* 21 June, 2007 http://www.theage.com.au/news/na-tional/public-backs-gay-unions-equality/2007/06/20/1182019204491.
html

[137] For a summary of this poll and the full poll results visit, http://www.
australianmarriageequality.com/releases/20090616.htm

[138] Dane, *op cit.*

[139] Previous studies within the gay, lesbian, bisexual and transgender
community in NSW and Victoria reflect the high and growing level
of support for same-sex marriage within the community. For more
see McNair, R., and N. Thomacos, Victorian Gay and Lesbian Rights
Lobby (with the assistance of Gay and Lesbian Health Victoria), *Not Yet
Equal, Report on the VGLRL same sex relationships survey,* 2005, p.38.
See: http://www.vglrl.org.au/files/publications/NotYetEqualFullReport.
pdf
Also Gay and Lesbian Rights Lobby, *All Love is Equal, Isn't It? The
recognition of same-sex relationships undear federal law, Consultation
Report,* February 2007, p. 17. See: http://glrl.org.au/images/stories/
all_love_is_equal_isnt_it.pdf

[140] This information supplied by the Senate Legal and Constitutional
Affairs Committee secretariat

[141] For a history of same-sex marriage in Australia, including the anteced-ents of the current debate, see "Marriage without a man: understanding
the emergence of same-sex marriage in Australia", an unpublished hon-ours thesis by Max Denton, presented in the School of Historical and
Philosophical Studies at the University of Melbourne, December 2014.

[142] see Willet, G., *Living Out Loud: a history of gay and lesbian activism in
Australia,* Allen and Unwin, Sydney, 2000, p8-9

[143] Branson-Potts, H., "A decades-old same-sex marriages complicates a
green-card case", *Los Angeles Times,* 1.6.2014, http://www.latimes.com/
nation/la-me-c1-gay-green-card-20140701-story.html#page=1

[144] Horan, A., Next step down the aisle is plain, Sydney Morning Herald, 12.02.2011, http://www.theage.com.au/it-pro/next-step-down-the-aisle-is-plain-20110211-1aqil.html

[145] Arndt, D., "World champ axeman backs gay marriage", Sydney Morning Herald, 9.9.2011

[146] Megalogenis, G., "Gillard and Abbott's bipartisanship on gay nuptials is based on a fallacy", The Australian, 17.12.2011

[147] Puplick, C., "Conscience votes should be a basic Liberal ideal", The Drum, 23.12.2014, http://www.abc.net.au/news/2014-12-23/puplick-conscience-vote-on-marriage-equality/5983792

[148] Greenwich, A., quoted in Lisa Cox, "Same-sex marriage laws could be amended ahead of High Court legal challenge", Canberra Times, http://www.canberratimes.com.au/act-news/samesex-marriage-laws-could-be-amended-ahead-of-high-court-legal-challenge-20131024-2w3xt.html

[149] Hinton-Teoh, I., interview with the author, 26.4.2015

[150] Vedantam, S., "Bans Of Same-Sex Marriage Can Take A Psychological Toll", NPR, 20.5.2013

[151] Ben Callegari, Psychologists for Marriage Equality, Submission to the Senate inquiry into the Marriage Equality Amendment Bill 2012 and the Marriage Amendment Bill 2012

[152] Barlow, F.K., Dane, S.K., Techakesari, P., & Stork-Brett. K. (2012). The psychology of same- sex marriage opposition: A preliminary findings report. School of Psychology. The University of Queensland.

[153] Same-Sex Marriage Research, Crosby/Textor Research, Sydney, 2014

[154] Rudd, K., "Church and State are able to have different positions on same sex marriage", 20.05.2013, http://www.kevinruddmp.com/2013/05/church-and-state-are-able-to-have.html

[155] Bourke, L., "Abbott government rising star Josh Frydenberg reveals switch on gay marriage position", The Age, 26.03.2015, http://www.smh.com.au/federal-politics/political-news/abbott-government-rising-star-josh-frydenberg-reveals-switch-on-gay-marriage-position-20150326-1m7wro.html

[156] "Gay marriage polls find personal relationships have major impact on support", Huffington Post, 21.03.2013

[157] For more on the science of storytelling see, Jonathan Gottschall, The Storytelling Animal, Houghton Mifflin, 2012, and, Brian Boyd, On the Origin of Stories: Evolution, Cognitio, and Fiction, Harvard University Press, 2009

[158] Bush, P., "Not Happy, Nicola", Webdiary blog, 10 aug. 2004, http://www.smh.com.au/ articles/2004/08/10/1092102440370.html

[159] Hughes, R., *The Fatal Shore*, Pan, Sydney, 1988, p246

[160] Alan Atkinson, "Convicts and courtship" in Patricia Grimshaw, Chris McConville and ellen Mcewen (eds), *Families in Colonial Australia*, allen & Unwin, Sydney, 1985, p. 25

[161] Atkinson, A., "Convicts and Courtship", in P. Grimshaw, C. McConville and E. McEwen, *Families in Colonial Australia*, Allen and Unwin, Sydney, 1985, pp20-25. Also see Patricia Russell (ed), *For Richer or Poorer: early colonial marriages*, Melbourne University Press, 1994, p6-7

[162] Kent, D., and N. Townsend, "Some Aspects of Colonial Marriage: a case study of the Swing Protesters", in *Labour History*, No 74, May 1988, University of Sydney Press

[163] Atkinson, op cit, p24

[164] Daniels, Kay., *Convict Women*, Allen & Unwin, Sydney, 1998, pp. 214 ff

[165] Tardiff, P., *Notorious Strumpets and Dangerous Girls*, Angus and Robertson, 1990

[166] See Babette Smith, *A Cargo of Women*, Rosenberg, Sydney, 2002, pp. 61 ff; Daniels, op cit; Atkinson op cit; and Kent and Townsend, op cit

[167] Wilson, S., "Language and ritual in marriage", in *The Push from the Bush: a bulletin of social history*, No 2, nov 1978, University of Western Australia, p98 and p103. Also see Atkinson, pp29-31

[168] Atkinson, *op cit*, p22

[169] Atkinson, *op cit*, p23

[170] Aveling, M., "She Only Married to be Free or Cleopatra Vindicated", in *The Push from the Bush: a bulletin of social history*, No 2, Nov 1978, University of Western Australia, p120

[171] For more on this see J Owen, *Mixed Matches: interracial marriage in Australia*, University of NSW Press, 1991, p34ff

[172] National Archives of Australia, "Mrs O'Keefe and the battle for White Australia", http://www.multiculturalaustralia.edu.au/doc/Brawley_AnnieOKeefe.pdf

[173] Brawley, S., "Mrs O'Keefe and the battle for White Australia", national Archives of Australia, 1.6.2006 http://www.naa.gov.au/Images/Brawley%20Oct%202007%20edit_tcm16-35888.pdf

[174] For more on the case of Gladys Namagu and Mick Daly see CA Hughes, "The marriage of Mick and Gladys: a discretion without an appeal", in in B. B. Schaffer and d. C. Corbett (eds), *Decisions: case studies in Australian administration*, 1965 (Australian public policy, 1981), and H Brook, "The Troubled Courtship of Gladys and Mick", *Australian Journal of Political Science*, v32, No. 3, 1997

[175] Ellinghaus, K., "Regulating Koori Marriages: The 1886 Victorian Aborigines Protection Act", *Journal of Australian Studies*, v. 67, 2001, p. 23. also, Richard Broome, *Aboriginal Victorians: A History since 1800*, Allen & Unwin, Sydney, 2005, p. 114.

[176] Reynolds, H., *Nowhere People: How International Race Thinking Shaped Australia's Identity*, Viking, Melbourne, 2005, p. 132.

[177] Chesterman, J., and B Galligan, "Citizens without rights" in *Aborigines and Australian Citizenship*, Cambridge University Press, Cambridge, 1997, p. 142. also, Katherine Ellinghaus, "Absorbing the 'Aboriginal Problem': controlling interracial marriage in australia in the late nineteenth and early twentieth centuries", *Journal of Aboriginal History*, v. 27, 2003, p. 186.

[178] Reynolds, *op cit* pp. 145 ff.

[179] Ellinghaus, *op cit* pp. 190 ff. Also, Reynolds, op cit p. 170.

[180] Haebich, A., *For Their Own Good: Aborigines and the Government in South West of Western Australia 1900-1940*, University of Western Australia Pres, 1988, p313

[181] recounted in Rajkowski, P., *Linden girl : a story of outlawed lives*, University of Western Australia Press, 1995

[182] recounted in Kinnane, S., *Shadow Lines*, Fremantle Press, Perth, 2003

[183] Attwood, B., and A. Markus, *The Struggle for Aboriginal Rights: a documentary history*, Allen and Unwin, Sydney, 1999, p130

[184] "Our Ten Points, Deputation to the Prime Minister", *Australian Abo Call*, No1, April 1938, in Attwood and Markus op cit, pp89-94

[185] For an example of the parallel emergence of references to Hitler and to the freedom to marry in the advocacy of Aboriginal activists see B Attwood and A Markus, *Thinking Black: William Cooper and the Australian Aborigines' League*, Aboriginal Studies Press 2005.

[186] Nicholson, A., "The 'reform' that shames Australia", *The Age*, 20.9.2004, http://www.theage.com.au/articles/2004/09/19/1095532174080.html. See also Ruth McNair, "Outcomes for Children Born of ART in a Diverse Range of Families: Occasional Paper", Victorian Law Reform Commission, Melbourne, 2004; Paul Hastings, Johanna Vyncke, Caroline Sullivan, Kelly McShane, Michael Benibgui and William Utendale, "Children's Development of Social Competence Across Family Types", Department of Justice, Ottawa, 2006; Charlotte Patterson, "Lesbian and Gay Parenting", American Psychological Association, Washington, 2005.

[187] Pope Francis, as reported in *The Independent*, London, 18.11.2014, http://www.independent.co.uk/news/world/europe/pope-francis-de-

clares-union-between-man-and-woman-at-root-of-marriage-in-blow-to-gay-rights-9867561.html

[188] Kiska, R., cited in the *Sydney Star Observer*, 26.10.2014, http://www.starobserver.com.au/news/local-news/acl-2014-national-conference-the-highs-and-the-lows/129333

[189] http://www.aph.gov.au/hansard/senate/commttee/S12538.pdf

[190] Bill Muehlenberg & Rodney Croome, *Why vs Why: gay marriage*, Pantera Press, Sydney, 2010, p55

[191] Ford, C., Same sex marriage needs straight people to take a stand in Australia, *WA Today* website, 3.2.2015, http://www.watoday.com.au/comment/same-sex-marriage-needs-straight-people-to-take-a-stand-in-australia-20150202-133krv.html

[192] Spade, D., and C Willse, "I still think marriage is the wrong goal" in *Against Equality: queer revolution not mere inclusion*, Conrad Ryan (ed), AK Press, Baltimore, 2014, p32

[193] Kean, J., "We should listen to Gillard on same-sex marriage", *ABC Drum website*, 2.10.2013, http://www.abc.net.au/news/2013-10-02/kean-julia-gillard-and-same-sex-marriage/4993640

[194] This reflection was made during a meeting with Julia Gillard when she was Prime Minister, attended by the author and a number of other marriage equality advocates.

[195] Kaufman MJ and K Miles, "Queer kids of queer parents against gay marriage", in, *Against Equality, op cit*, p82-83

[196] Altman, D., *The Homosexualization of America*, St Martin's Press, NY, 1982, p187

[197] Altman, D., *AIDS in the Mind of America*, Doubleday, NY, 1986, p159

[198] ibid, p188

[199] David McWhirter and Andrew Mattison, *The Male Couple: How Relationships Develop*. Englewood Cliffs, New Jersey: Prentice-Hall, 1984, pp. 252-253.

[200] Ettelbrick, P., "Since When Is Marriage a Path to Liberation?", in William Rubenstein, ed., Lesbians, Gay Men and the Law, The New Press, New York, 1993, pp. 401-405

[201] Dessaix, R., "Robert Dessaix on the case against gay marriage", *The Sydney Morning Herald*, 1.11.2014, http://www.smh.com.au/good-weekend/robert-dessaix-on-the-case-against-gay-marriage-20141101-116vlb.html

[202] Kennicott, P., A memoir of gay male literature, *Smuggler* website, Autumn, 2014, http://www.vqronline.org/memoir-articles/2014/10/smuggler

[203] Rogers, T., Edmund White comes out swinging, Salon, 15.10.2015, http://www.salon.com/2009/10/15/edmund_white_interview/

[204] Rundle, G., "*The Drum*, gay marriage and knowing your history", Crikey websitehttp://www.crikey.com.au/2011/12/08/the-dum-gay-marriage-and-knowing-your-history/

[205] Altman, D., quoted in "Gay marriage 'self-indulgent crap'", Sydney Star Observer, 20.4.2008, http://www.starobserver.com.au/news/local-news/new-south-wales-news/gay-marriage-selfindulgent-crap/11847

[206] Pilger, J., Gay marriage is a distraction: remember Manning, *ABC The Drum*, 18.5.2012, http://www.abc.net.au/news/2012-05-18/pilger-manning-not-gay-marriage-is-the-issue/4017816

[207] Sharlet, J., "Inside the Iron Closet: What It's Like to Be Gay in Putin's Russia", *GQ*, February 2014, http://www.gq.com/news-politics/big-issues/201402/being-gay-in-russia

[208] Dick, T., "Marriage equality key to expunging homophobia", *Brisbane Times*, 25.2.15, http://www.brisbanetimes.com.au/comment/marriage-equality-key-to-expunging-homophobia-20150224-13mlxt.html

[209] Kate and Deeg, "Marriage is still the opiate of the queers", in *Against Equality*, op cit, p48

[210] Ross, A., Berlin Story: How the Germans invented gay rights—more than a century ago, *The New Yorker*, 26.1.2015, http://www.newyorker.com/magazine/2015/01/26/berlin-story

[211] Interview with Ryan Conrad, 13.1.2012, *Daily Xtra*, http://dailyxtra.com/canada/news/the-marrying-kind-51542

[212] Jagose, A., "The trouble with gay marriage", *The Conversation*, 7.11.2013, http://theconversation.com/the-trouble-with-gay-marriage-19196

[213] Curtis Red, "Nothing Civil About Our Unions", *Farrago*, Melbourne University Student Union, Melbourne, 2008

[214] Metz, T., Untying the Knot: Marriage, the State, and the Case for Their Divorce, Princeton University Press, New Jersey, 2010 http://www.amazon.com/Untying-Knot-Marriage-State-Divorce/dp/069112667